PRAISE FOR
CORPORATE INNOVATION IN THE FIFTH ERA

"Le Merle and Davis have really hit the mark with *Corporate Innovation in the Fifth Era* – they have managed to capture the essential dynamics that got us here and the innovation imperative that we must all embrace to move forward, particularly the notion that the C-team must view and act on innovation as a must-have priority. In 20+ years of working with top teams throughout Silicon Valley and the world, I've seen again and again that it is the mindsets and orientation of senior executives that catalyze change in the systems they lead. Not only do they understand this and the challenges associated with it, they thoughtfully lay out a process for how to do it."

Andrew Blum, CEO/Managing Partner Trium Group

"This book is a truly stimulating narrative that creatively connects the dots and contextualizes human behavior. It is a must-read for any business student, CEO or general public (it's a fun, fast whirlwind of a read) interested in the effects of technology (both digital and biotech) on our world. It inspired me to not only think differently about the local and global worlds we live in, but possible ways of thinking about their connectivity, as we actively participate as engaged citizens in the creation of our future."

Cari Borja, Anthropologist

"Must-read for corporate executives and individuals focused on creating wealth by leveraging breakthroughs in technology innovation in the 'Fifth Era.' Provides practical, actionable, tools and techniques for instilling a sustainable internal innovation strategy and culture in corporate environments, as well as a comprehensive toolkit to access and leverage external innovation."

Patrick Byrne, Investor/Board Member,
Former Senior Partner Accenture/A.T. Kearney

"One of those rare business books that is consistently thought-provoking while also being pragmatic in suggesting actions that corporate leaders can implement straight away. And it is an easy and fun book to read too."

Ranjana Clark, Bay Area President/Head of Transaction Banking
Americas Mitsubishi UFJ Financial Group

"Matthew and Alison's immersion in entrepreneurialism as investors, advisors and board members over 20+ years affords them unique insights into the strategies companies must embrace to prepare for and leverage disruptive innovations that will emerge from the confluence of digital and biotechnology.

Coupled with empirical evidence from top innovators including Apple, Google/Alphabet and Microsoft, *Corporate Innovation in the Fifth Era* provides pragmatic guidance relevant to everyone from entrepreneurs, investors and business leaders to those seeking strategies to participate in this next phase of unprecedented growth and value creation."

Shirley Foster, VP Mobile Engineering
American Express

"The secret sauce that makes a consistently successful innovative company is one of the most explored and least understood questions the business elite is confronted with when preparing for the digital revolution. This is now changing with this book: in 250 pages it gives them – and you - the insights they would pay millions of dollars for."

Dr. Roman Friedrich, Managing Director AlixPartners

"Le Merle and Davis draw on their wealth of experience to produce a book that synthesizes how and why companies succeed, and fail, in today's innovation-centric economy. A book that should be widely read by all those attempting to navigate the Fifth Era."

Tim Jenkinson, Professor of Finance
Oxford University

"An excellent job of presenting what the subtitle calls 'lessons from the most innovative companies'. The book is comprehensive providing societal and geopolitical perspectives as context for specific examples and suggestions for corporate leaders to drive innovation."

Philipp Jung, Chief Strategy Officer HP Inc.

"The authors have been focused on innovation for most of their working careers. They clearly outline the lessons they have learned as investors, advisors and board directors and share pragmatic suggestions for ways that leaders can take action."

Aliza Knox, COO Unlockd, Formerly VP AsiaPacific Twitter

"If you are looking for a blueprint to support your company's innovation strategy—this book is it. It delivers a powerful one-two punch because it provides context and perspective into the cultural drivers that shape change and enable growth. It also delivers the specific necessary steps leaders need to adopt to compete. This book should be required reading for MBA students and current business leaders."

Debbie Kristofferson, VP Marketing Drip Drop Hydration, Former VP Peets/Walmart.com

"How could any business person not be interested in learning the lessons of the most innovative and most valuable companies in the world? This book is full of pragmatic suggestions for readying companies for a new world of disruptive innovations."

Janet Lamkin, Bank Executive

"In a world of continuous, convulsive change, Le Merle and Davis cut through the fog with a compelling assessment of the big change drivers and how they will shape the new challenges and opportunities ahead. This tour de force is a must-read for anyone who wants to succeed in a confused and troubled world."

Paul Laudicina, Chairman Global Business Policy Council, Chairman Emeritus, A.T. Kearney

"This book contains a great selection of lessons learned by some of the world's largest and most profitable companies. Learning how and why those lessons lead to successful innovation is the key – and this book is a front row seat."

Dan'l Lewin, Corporate Vice President Technology/ Civic Engagement Microsoft

"The authors paint a compelling and provocative picture of the next era for business, when compounding innovations fundamentally disrupt the world. Fasten your seatbelts for when Generation C (those born digital after 1990) take charge. Le Merle and Davis provide an easily readable and practical guide to the wild ride ahead."

Lenny Mendonca, Retired Senior Partner McKinsey and Company

"This book offers business leaders a well-defined, articulate toolkit for cultivating corporate innovation. It takes a refreshing, long-term look at humanity's innovation, combining business and case studies with the authors' experiences and observations of broader trends."

Christopher Pencavel, GM Zesty

"Le Merle and Davis have given us that most precious of commodities – a book that genuinely makes you sit back and think. Yes, it probably has great value in the world of corporate finance. The zeitgeist of corporate innovation is both seductive and compelling, but it has equal value for policy makers. It highlights that, in the move to a Fifth Era, the train with carriages marked 'global connectivity', 'automation' and 'corporate wealth creation' has left the station. And that dealing with the social challenges of wealth (re)distribution, of mass unemployment in traditional labor markets, and of a global shift in the geo-strategic economic power base is the political challenge of the 21st century."

Lieutenant General Nick Pope, Deputy Chief of the General Staff, British Army

"This book persuasively shows the risk to companies that fail to innovate, and the importance of embedding innovation deeply in corporate strategy. It also goes further, providing tools and pathways that can help companies design and execute innovation strategies. While the term innovation is over-used, its importance is growing as economic change accelerates. Le Merle and Davis provide a service by distilling the process to its essentials, and presenting it in a practical and highly accessible narrative."

Sean Randolph, Senior Director Bay Area Council Economic Institute

"Alison Davis and Matthew Le Merle bring three critical credentials to this authoritative and accessible handbook on how to explore and exploit in the era of disruption, the power of empirical evidence with numerous case studies to authenticate their insights, the virtue of their location which is the world's game-changing centre of gravity, and their parentage of five splendid Generation C(licker)'s.

For the corporation making better bets on the future this is a must-read; likewise for humankind wanting to speed date this future."

Ruth Richardson, Principal Ruth Richardson [NZ] Ltd,
Former New Zealand Minister of Finance

"At Alphabet and Google, we work with companies of all sizes around the world. The desire to enable and capitalize on innovation is a unifying theme for all of them. This book will help senior executives and board members lead their companies in this new era of faster change and innovation."

Allan Thygesen, President Americas Google,
Lecturer Stanford Graduate School of Business

"Even the most innovative companies usually stagnate and then die as scale and complexity come to defeat their innovative capacities. *Corporate Innovation in the Fifth Era* provides a deep analysis of the barriers to innovation and most importantly the strategies for overcoming those barriers. Le Merle and Davis have given every business leader concerned with innovation in large organizations a powerful set of tools for driving that innovation to fruition."

Peter Schwartz, SVP Strategic Planning Salesforce

"Le Merle and Davis have been focused on innovation in Silicon Valley for 30 years. This book shares with everyone the lessons they have learned as investors, advisors and board directors. Very insightful and pragmatic suggestions for readying companies for a new world of disruptive innovations."

Carola Wahl, CTMO AXA Switzerland,
Member of the Board AXA Strategic Ventures

"Thought-provoking and entertaining. A 'must-read' for any C suite executive or board member interested in innovation!"

John Wilson, President Hyannis Port Capital,
Former COO Gap and President Staples International

CORPORATE
INNOVATION
IN THE FIFTH ERA

Also by Matthew C. Le Merle and Alison Davis

Build Your Fortune in the Fifth Era

CORPORATE
INNOVATION
IN THE FIFTH ERA

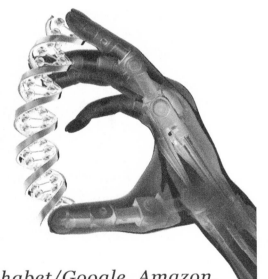

Lessons from Alphabet/Google, Amazon,
Apple, Facebook and Microsoft

MATTHEW C. LE MERLE
AND ALISON DAVIS

First Printing 2017

ISBN: 978-0-9861613-7-7 (paperback K)
ISBN: 978-0-9861613-8-4 (hardbound)
ISBN: 978-0-9861613-9-1 (paperback X)

Library of Congress Cataloging-in-Publication Data is available.

This work was designed and printed in the United States of America by

145 Corte Madera Town Center, #415
Corte Madera, CA 94924

www.CartwrightPublishing.com
415-250-6343

Cartwright Publishing is a publisher of business and professional books. We help entrepreneurs, business leaders and professionals share their stories, passion and knowledge to help others. If you have a manuscript or book idea that you would like us to consider for publishing, please visit CartwrightPublishing.com

Cover design: Katherine Masters
Interior design: Sue Balcer

wild(at our first)beasts uttered human words
- our second coming made stones sing like birds –
but o the starhushed silence which our thirds's

-ee cummings

For Joyce and Jack, Linda and Claud
With gratitude for your gift of life in this astonishing time

Visit CorporateInnovationInTheFifthEra.com
to receive free book updates, additional content about topics
in this book, and find out more about the authors.

A Note from the Authors

Part 1 of this book has been included in its entirety in our companion work:

Build Your Fortune in the Fifth Era

For those of our readers who have read this book, we recommend you proceed to Part 2.

Table of Contents

Table of Exhibits

Table of Sidebars

Introduction

Many leaders of big organizations, I think, don't believe that change is possible. But if you look at history, things do change, and if your business is static, you're likely to have issues.

—Larry Page

It was a beautiful Napa Valley day in 2009 with the sun beating down on the grapevines as far as the eye could see. We had been invited to speak at a forum of 25 or so corporate venture executives from America's leading companies hosted by Silicon Valley Bank. The topic was emerging trends in corporate innovation. We were the session after lunch—the slot when everyone is full of lunch and feeling more like having a nap than listening to another speaker.

Best then to start with questions to get their participation.

1. Over the next decade where will the most important innovations in your industry come from?
    a. Your own company
    b. Your own industry
    c. Outside your industry
2. What percentage of your innovation spend is internal vs. external—people and capital?
3. What percentage of your innovation spend focuses beyond your industry?

This seems to work and the attendees become engaged in the topic. No one believes their company will be the disruptive innovator, and instead, the group is split equally between those who believe the disruptors will be from within versus from outside their industries.

Most of the group says their companies are spending between 70% and 90% of their innovation resources (people and capital) internally and that these corporate venture teams get a fraction of the total corporate resources to spend externally. But almost none of that is being spent beyond the narrow defines of their industry. No one is scouting from truly disruptive innovations attacking from beyond their industry.

Here's the bottom line that emerges: corporate resources are not aligned with the likely sources of disruptive innovation—even when the corporate strategy is saying that innovation is the most important priority on the CEO's agenda, as it is at all of these companies.

The message of our book is that we are living in a time of dramatic transition between the Industrial Era and a new Fifth Era being driven by the Digital Revolution, Biotechnology Revolution, and a host of other disruptive technologies —more than the world has ever seen at work at one time – that will transform the way humans exist on the planet. Enormous value is already being created in this transition by companies in many industries that are able to leverage these new technologies to create powerful products and services that customers relate to and value. Enormous value is also being lost as existing companies are superseded and are not able to regain their position with customers. The stakes are high on corporate innovation and are only getting higher. The most important strategic question in most industries is how to leverage new technologies to increase relevance to customers, efficiency and competitiveness in a rapidly changing world and how to avoid being displaced. And we are immersed in a transformation that is only just beginning.

Jumping forward to 2015 and we are conducting another corporate innovation forum, this time to leaders of some of the largest banks in the world who have come to the heart of Silicon Valley to learn. We ask the same questions. We get the same answers as in 2009. Six years have gone by, and we have seen little change at the macro-level in how many of the world's largest companies are approaching corporate innovation.

Meanwhile, in the same timeframe the world's most innovative companies are surging ahead, obsessed with delivering value to their customers and with how new technologies can be harnessed to accomplish that. Many companies that didn't exist in 2009 are now household names and have multibillion-dollar valuations.

For 30 years, we have lived and worked in the US – mostly in Silicon Valley, first coming from London and Yorkshire in the UK as young professionals to pursue MBAs at Harvard and Stanford Universities, then working as management consultants at McKinsey & Company, AT Kearney, Monitor Group, and Booz & Company. Following that, we took on corporate roles as SVP Global Strategy and Marketing at Gap Inc. and as Chief Financial Officer at Barclays Global Investors, the world's largest institutional investment management firm. More recently, we also did stints in private equity and venture capital as venture partner and private equity general partner at Monitor Ventures and Belvedere Capital respectively. Over the last 20 years, we have transitioned to becoming board directors and advisors to fast growth private companies as well as larger public companies that are working hard to stay relevant, as well as angel investors in dozens of early stage companies.

During these years we have become immersed in innovation and entrepreneurialism. We have helped large corporations become better at innovation, we have invested in and supported start-ups that have launched disruptive innovations, and we have advised countries and regions on being in the flow of innovation. We are surrounded by many of the most remarkable disruptions of our time and by the exhilarating new digital world that is being built around us. And because of our work and location, we have been fortunate to be able to observe at close quarters the practices of many of the world's innovation leaders and to witness the incredible value creation that has resulted.

In writing this book we have attempted to synthesize the lessons we have learned about operating at the frontier of innovation - lessons from companies such as Alphabet/Google, Amazon.com (Amazon), Apple, Facebook, and Microsoft - and also from many other innovators we have been fortunate to work with as advisors, investors, board directors and employees. Almost all of the examples we cite are from our personal experience – although in some cases we have added secondary research and cases studies where we have found it useful to do so. We have condensed these lessons into a new approach to corporate innovation that we believe is better suited to the Fifth Era.

This book outlines the nature of the transition we are in from the Fourth to the Fifth Era and describes many of the disruptive innovations and the impact they are having. We show why a new approach to corporate innovation is required and we outline many of the most important steps that should be taken by those responsible for driving innovation in their firms. The book provides insights into how the most valuable companies in the world are fueling their success with a new corporate innovation approach, and it also demonstrates the substantial risks of not embracing this new era comprehensively - the companies losing economic value most quickly are among those who most need the lessons provided in this book.

We wrote this book to be relevant for everyone who is responsible for the innovation processes of their company or organization – as a senior executive, board director, advisor, and also for everyone working in an organization that is striving to stay relevant in a rapidly changing world.

This book should also give food for thought to others in the innovation and entrepreneurship ecosystem – universities, think tanks, capital providers, governments, service providers, advisors and many others.

We hope you enjoy reading it and we wish you the best as you strive to help your organizations thrive and prosper in the Fifth Era.

Matthew C. Le Merle
Alison Davis
Tiburon, California, USA

Part 1 | The Fifth Era

Chapter 1
Past Is Prologue – The First Four Eras

Study the past if you would divine the future.

—Confucius

Decades ago, few would have been able to imagine just how different the world would be today. Three decades ago, we were largely unconnected from one another. It took time to create, share, or find data and content, and we relied upon physical means to do so. To innovate, manufacture, market, and distribute their products companies and industries relied upon approaches that had, in some cases, gone unchanged for many decades. Information was to be found in libraries, archives, and desk drawers if you knew where to look.

In just 30 years, all of that has changed.

Today, we are connected, information is broadly available and easy to find, innovation is quick and iterative, and innovators are able to access the latest technologies and tools wherever they are across the globe. Today, most companies conduct their businesses in fundamentally different ways, providing cheaper, better, and faster products to their customers, and this is only the beginning. As new technologies continue to emerge and innovation continues to disrupt, we will build upon the foundations, laid out just twenty five years ago with the creation of the Internet and the digital economy, to launch ourselves into a Fifth Era of economic activity.

In order to better understand just how dramatically different this Fifth Era might be, we think that it is worthwhile to begin this book by briefly reviewing the four eras of human activity that have gone before to see how disruptive innovations were able to change the very essence of human activity around the world and the opportunities that this created for new wealth creation.

While each of the four eras of human activity was very different in nature, there are some common themes that will be relevant as we look at the coming Fifth Era. First, that disruptive innovations are able to fundamentally change the essence of the way that most people spend their time. Second, that new and very different wealth-creation opportunities surface as human activity adjusts to the new era and the activities that characterize it. Third, that this wealth creation does not automatically accrue to the best-positioned and most successful players of the prior era. And finally, that it is possible to see a new era coming and position yourself for the next phase of wealth creation, but that this has to be a distinct choice: prior wealth-creation strategies may not be relevant in the subsequent era.

The four eras that we will briefly cover are the **Hunter-Gatherer Era**, which began in times long past—perhaps 2.5 million years ago—and began to give way to the next era between 12,000 and 11,000 years ago. As with other subsequent eras, we still see vestiges of foraging societies in remote parts of the world today. However, the vast majority of humans have moved on into other ways of spending their time. We will then briefly look at the **Agrarian Era**, which began about 11,000 years ago and continued roughly until the beginning of the fifteenth century AD. We will then turn to the **Mercantile Era**, which came to be the dominant economic mode between 1400 and 1800 when the world became, for the first time, a connected trading environment. Finally, we will review the **Industrial Era**, which was launched with the first industrial revolution in the mid-nineteenth century and passed through three distinct phases culminating in today's industrialized world.

While there is a great deal of overlap between these four eras, and in each subsequent era some peoples and groups continued to live by the rules of the prior era(s), nonetheless, the center of gravity and the driving force of human society is quite distinct in each era. So today, we still see foragers in the rainforest and tundra, agrarian communities on most continents, and mercantile traders everywhere—but the dominant theme of the last two centuries has been that of an industrialized world.

Each of these four eras was supplanted by dramatic innovations that enabled society to move into a new phase of existence, and it is these disruptive innovations that we are beginning to see surfacing at an increasingly rapid rate, giving us confidence that the fourth era is beginning to close and the Fifth Era is about to arrive. However, the time of transition between eras can be measured in generations and is always messy—we are living in the time of transition between the Industrial and Fifth Eras today, and no one can be sure exactly what the future will hold. What we can be sure of is that the Fifth Era will create exciting new wealth-creation opportunities just as each new era did in times past.

Exhibit 1

The Five Eras

Era	Name	Span	Disruptive Innovations
1	Hunter/ Gatherer	— to 11,000 BC	—

2	Agrarian	11,000 BC to ±1400 AD	• Domestication
			  –First high productivity crops
			  – Local Animal Husbandry
			• Irrigation
			• Farming Tools
			• Storage

3	Mercantile	±1400 AD to ±1800 AD	• Great global convergence and new forms of transportation • Columbian exchange of plants and animals • Global economy with common forms of currency and methods of exchange
4	Industrial	±1800 AD to ±2000 AD	Initially: • Steam Engine • Blast Furnaces • Early machine tools Then: • Electricity • Steel Finally: • Computers
5	Fifth Era	±2000 AD	• Digital Revolution • Biotechnology • Others

Source: Fifth Era, LLC

The Hunter-Gatherer Era

From the ancient past up until about 11,000 or 12,000 years ago, most people on the face of the earth lived by hunting and gathering in a subsistence economy. Some researchers also call this the Forager Era, and there are groups of people who still rely upon this way of living today. In the ancient past, people lived by gathering and collecting the abundance of nature: hunting and trapping big and small game, fishing and gathering shellfish, and making use of whatever plant foods they could find. Most hunters and gatherers combined these various types of food acquisition. They varied their forms of foraging depending upon the seasons, the movements and availability of animals, and the natural cycles of harvesting opportunities.

Most of these hunter-gatherer cultures were close to subsistence communities, and typically only small surpluses could be gathered and saved for periods of scarcity. Certain plants could be kept without spoiling, some animal products might be dried and stored, but for the most part, the community relied upon the availability of the moment.

Throughout this first era the dominant societal mode was a tribal group—a band of people who would collaborate, work together, and help each other—often tied together by blood in extended family groups. Typically, they would rely upon the local environment for their needs, and if they did exhaust the local environment, they might need to be nomadic, either on a continuous or an episodic basis. Groups were small in number, typically 100 or less, and there was very little ability to create permanent settlements. Continuous foraging in the same space was rarely feasible, so settlements would be periodically abandoned in all but the most fruitful places.

Whether you subscribe to Thomas Hobbes' view of 1651, that the lives of hunter-gathers were "solitary, poor, nasty, brutish and short" or prefer the view that Marshall Sahlins proffered in the 1960s, that, rather, they were the "original affluent society" with most of their time reserved for leisure, what is sure is that they were unable to accumulate much in the way of material wealth. Wealth creation was limited with most individuals being active foragers in a small-group setting. Few were able to accumulate significantly more than the average of their group—leaders of groups might accumulate more spare time by asking others to forage on their behalf and might share a disproportionate part of the group's possessions. But, to a large extent, accumulation of wealth was not possible.

During this era, the world's population grew to perhaps 4 million by the arrival of the second great era.

No surpluses meant no accumulation of material wealth in the hands of the rich.

The Agrarian Era

Some 11,000 years ago we see the widespread arrival of a new Agrarian Era. While some limited farming had certainly existed for thousands of years before, in a relatively short timeframe of a few thousand years we see the appearance of farming as the dominant paradigm on almost every continent with the exception of Australia. And while some peoples continued to hunt and gather, the majority became dependent upon planned agricultural activities for most of their needs.

The disruptive innovations that displaced foraging with agriculture were created as the result of some thousands of years of experimentation as farmers sought to improve the yields they could produce from the land they tended. They did this by creating more productive and reliable crops and breeding more productive animals, thus becoming ever better at domestication. They created better and better tools with which to farm, and they learned the essentials of irrigation, mass harvesting, and the storing of their surplus produce. The combination of many individual innovations drove the Agrarian Era forward.

The first major period of disruptive change that we have a record of is the so-called First Agricultural Revolution, which is also named the Neolithic Revolution after historian V. Gordon Childe (1929). This was a period, particularly in the Middle East, when animal husbandry and crop farming techniques reached a point of development that, when combined with better irrigation technologies, allowed for much higher yields and much higher density of population. In those parts of the world impacted, foraging was largely displaced by settled agrarian communities that then focused on further improving their farming technologies and practices.

A Second Agricultural Revolution, or a Medieval Green Revolution, began around the eighth century in the Islamic world, where very high-producing crops appear to have emerged for the first time, including wheat, rice, cotton, and sorghum (Watson, 1974). Again, with the help of irrigation, these four staple crops appear to have dramatically changed the way that society progressed and also, for the first time, gave the opportunity for people to accumulate wealth, primarily through the ownership of land and the leadership of communities.

The second agrarian phase saw the beginning of the rise of large, well-organized empires. In particular, the three largest of the period between 1000 BC and 500 AD: the Persian Achaemenid Empire, the Han Empire in China, and the Roman Empire. These empires also became the locus for wealth capture driven by their ruling elites, however they rose to power.

These three, and many other smaller empires developed powerful military forces and mercantile and trading skills to expand their reach and to influence other agrarian people to support their expansion. The vast majority of people living in this period were living on the land as farmers, however, the existence of soldiers, merchants, traders, and other specialized service providers became widespread.

Fueled by these disruptive agrarian innovations, the population of the world began to increase rapidly—from perhaps 4 million some 11,000 years ago to around 450 million at the end of the second era in 1400.

Exhibit 2
World Population Curve

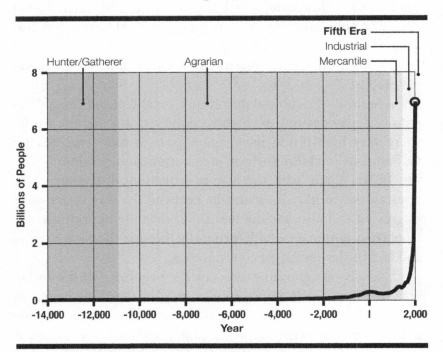

Source: United Nations Data Sheet, 2016; Fifth Era, LLC

In Europe, a final phase of the Agrarian Era began in the eighteenth century by which time the Mercantile Era was firmly established. The enclosing of the commons, the arrival of new techniques for planting and harvesting crops, and the continuing rollout of new crop rotation, irrigation, and stock-breeding technologies greatly increased farming productivity. The concentration of the owner-ship of land in this timeframe gave rise to very significant wealth creation fixed in the hands of the European landed gentry.

However, by then most nations had discovered a much more productive way to focus their efforts: the Mercantile Era.

The Mercantile Era

In the Agrarian Era, the primary locus of wealth creation was the ownership of land and the control of the surpluses that that land was yielding. By the Mercantile Era, which begins around 1400, we see much more emphasis on trade and wealth being created by those that were able to participate in and control the exchange of goods around the world.

The disruptive innovations of this period that ushered in the new era were threefold. First, we see the great global convergence in which new and sophisticated transportation and communica-tion approaches linked every continent. The age of sail allowed long-distance trading to take place on the world's oceans and the great sea-trading nations—England, France, Holland, Portugal, and Spain, among others—rose to prominence and their mer-chants and sovereigns accumulated great wealth.

This great global convergence, in turn, gave rise to the second disruptive innovation of this period—the Columbian exchange of plants, animals, and microorganisms between continents. In a very short period of time, the breakthrough innovations of do-mestication that had taken place in an unlinked fashion in the thousands of years before were suddenly shared. The Europeans got the potato and corn (maize), the Americans got the goat and wheat, and so on. In every part of the world, great increases in productivity occurred—although destructive microorganisms and diseases were also shared to the detriment of some societies, especially in the Americas.

The combination of these two great innovations led to the third breakthrough innovation of the Mercantile Era—the creation of a global economy with common forms of currency and accepted ways to exchange goods in marketplaces. Silver and gold became widely accepted, and the merchants and merchant houses scoured the world for opportunities to buy low and sell high, moving goods at great risk between the sellers and the buyers that they connected. With the help of large sailing vessels, they could do this at scale—not just the goods that could be packed on the backs of a camel caravan or ox-pulled cart.

Adam Smith (1776) coined the term "mercantile system" to describe how the early mercantile states worked to enrich themselves by restricting imports while working to expand their exports. This created a favorable balance of trade that would bring gold and silver into the state to the benefit of the mercantile elites. Following this pattern, Europe, in particular, saw the creation of wealthy trading cities and powerful organizations, such as the East India Company.

The Mercantile Era also saw the creation of military power on a scale not seen before as trading nations sought to secure their trading routes and extend their influence over the endpoints of their trading networks. The rise of the scientific method during the Scientific Revolution and the Enlightenment of this Mercantile Era also laid the groundwork for the coming Industrial Era. Science was now able to move faster than ever without the constraints of religious and political beliefs that had before made experimentation and innovation often hazardous to the health of the innovator. Just as the Mercantile Era saw the global trading of goods, it also saw a first global exchange of ideas.

The world's population grew from some 450 million to 1.3 billion by 1800, the next major time of transition.

The wealth creation of the Mercantile Era did not accrue automatically to those societies and leaders who had risen to prominence in the Agrarian Era. Indeed, the great empires of Asia, the Middle East, and to some extent the Americas were slow to adjust to the realities of the Mercantile Era and the need to master new transportation and trading innovations. Instead, the wealth creation of the era went to those who moved quickly to master these new innovations—the new merchants and merchant states.

The Industrial Era

The Industrial Era is the fourth era that we will review, beginning in the mid-eighteenth century and bringing us to today. The Industrial Era has passed through three distinct phases, each of which illustrates our core theme—disruptive innovations drive us forward and in so doing produce great wealth-creation opportunities for those who choose to master the new realities.

The first phase of disruption within the Industrial Era was the great Industrial Revolution of the mid-eighteenth century. Disruptive innovations, like the spinning jenny and spinning mule in textiles, the stationary steam engine, the blast furnace, and early machine tools, dramatically increased productivity. These early breakthroughs were accelerated by a shift in the types of energy that society used from biomass-based energy—primarily burning wood—to the age of coal and steam. These fossil fuels allowed much more efficient generation of energy and, with the invention and continuous development of the steam engine, allowed human beings to become much more effective in the ways that they created products and services. The steam engine was used to power machinery across almost every manufacturing sector, allowing faster production of greater quantities of merchandise.

This first Industrial Revolution also saw the creation of the factory and workhouse, and it was not without opposition—Ned Ludd and his Luddites being foremost in opposing the application of disruptive technologies in this new Industrial Era.

This first phase of the Industrial Era was accompanied by a very substantial increase in world population that had been building during the Mercantile Era. By the end of the nineteenth century, the world's population was approaching two billion people. So, the Industrial Revolution saw a compounding of factors—a much larger world population and a fundamental transformation in the way that those people worked, produced and lived.

The wealth creation of this period was primarily captured by the early industrialists and by those who applied new steam-based manufacturing approaches to existing industries, displacing manpower with machine power. These new manufacturing businesses were capital-intensive and, in many cases, family-owned businesses that needed additional capital influxes in order to compete. In this period we see the rise to supremacy of the corporate model of business, with companies owned by groups of shareholders raising capital from public markets and deploying it into expanding their operations. This is the model that continues as the dominant model in most places today.

The second phase of the Industrial Era, beginning around 1850, was driven by three new disruptive innovations—the widespread use of steel assisted by the invention of new mass steel furnaces by Sir Henry Bessemer, the arrival of electrical power, and the invention of mass production approaches beginning to be deployed at scale after the Great War (WW1). The corporate model continued to expand as more and more capital became available through the public markets. The development of national corporate champions then gave way in the mid-twentieth century to the development of multinational companies, capturing economies of scale and scope to dominate their target industries.

Despite two world wars and many smaller wars, the Industrial Era moved forward, and the world population continued to grow rapidly.

During the second half of the twentieth century, a large proportion of business activity was organized and managed within the four walls of the large public corporations. This is particularly true for innovation, where, beginning perhaps 100 years ago, corporate laboratories and R&D centers became increasingly important in driving innovations that would be utilized by the companies in their products and services.

The wealth creation of this timeframe was captured by corporate leaders and titans and by the financiers that backed them. Those who ran large corporations and those who played the capital financing games of the public markets captured most of the wealth creation of this phase.

The third major phase of the Industrial Era, termed the "Computer Age," is a result of the application of ever more powerful computing innovations to industrial activities. As we will show in the next section, we should make a clear distinction between the application of computing to established Industrial Era approaches and businesses versus the use of computing power to disrupt and replace these same businesses. In the Computer Age, as it applies to the third phase of the Industrial Era, the application of computer technologies to the activities of most large corporations around the world resulted in increases in their productivity.

However, computerization also unleashed a greatly increased rate of innovation and has enabled a new generation of innovators beyond the four walls of the industrial corporation. This has given rise to a new wave of disruptive innovations appearing at an accelerating pace, impacting every industry around the world.

In this era, the world's population expanded rapidly from 1.3 billion in 1800 to today's 7.5 billion.

Divining the Future

Over the last tens of thousands of years, we have seen at least four distinct eras of human activity on the surface of the earth. These four eras, the Hunter-Gatherer Era, the Agrarian Era, the Mercantile Era, and the Industrial Era, all share common themes.

1. First, disruptive innovations are able to fundamentally change the essence of the way that most people spend their time.
2. Second, new and very different wealth-creation opportunities surface as human activity adjusts to the new era and the activities that characterize it.
3. Third, this wealth creation does not automatically accrue to the best-positioned and most successful players of the prior era.
4. And finally, it is possible to see a new era coming and position yourself for the next phase of wealth creation, but this has to be a distinct choice: prior wealth-creation strategies may not be relevant in the subsequent era.

This is why we say the past is prologue.

Today disruptive innovations are coming at an ever-increasing rate. They are fundamentally displacing the "paradigm" of the fourth Industrial Era. Thomas Kuhn explained in his famous 1962 treatise *The Structure of Scientific Revolutions* that scientific paradigm shifts occur when some recognized problem of science, which has not been solved before, not only can be solved within a new paradigm but that the new paradigm also is able to preserve a relatively large part of the problem-solving that has been accomplished in the prior paradigm. When a new paradigm is able to do this, a shift occurs.

Today the disruptive innovations are surfacing at an ever-increasing rate, which we will detail in the next chapter. They are not only solving heretofore fundamental challenges of the Industrial Era, but they are able to do so while also holding onto the progress of that Era. They are meeting, essentially, the test that Kuhn created but are doing so at the societal level, not just at the level of a scientific breakthrough.

As we seek to understand the Fifth Era, the words of Confucius that began this chapter are important: "Study the past if you would divine the future."

In the next chapter, we will catalog a sample of the new innovations and the disruptive impacts they represent. Then, in the third chapter, we will combine them and show how this is the arrival of a new era of human activity.

Chapter 2
Disruptive Innovation Ushering in a New Era

The historian of science may be tempted to exclaim that when paradigms change, the world itself changes with them.

—*Thomas Kuhn*

The transition from one era to another has always been initiated and driven by disruptive innovations that have enabled society to fundamentally change the focus of activity and have produced new beneficiaries of wealth creation. But, the time of transition between eras is not quick and straightforward. It is a messy period that may extend over generations and which sees false starts, dead ends, and may advance faster in one place than another. The time of transition is, however, a period of dramatic transformation and wealth creation.

Do all disruptive innovations transform society to the level of an era change? Far from it. Most disruptive innovations occur within the context of a specific era. They improve and change the practices of that era, but they don't push it into a new era. The process of disruptive innovation is continuous, and most innovations provide incremental changes, which move society forward but don't challenge the very nature of the era in which they are born and established.

So, as observers of innovation, how would we know if the disruptive innovations we are observing are sufficient to herald a transition in eras? How would we know if we were in the time of transition?

Let's take an empirical look at today's disruptive innovations and ask the question, "Are these innovations incremental, or are they so disruptive as to be the heralds of a time of transition between eras?" This chapter does this first by looking at the innovations of the second half of the Industrial Era, next by considering the most recent innovations of the last thirty years, and then by observing the next waves of innovations that are beginning to surface. The aim of this chapter is to answer that question by demonstrating that we are shifting into a very disruptive phase of innovation that heralds the arrival of an entirely new era: the Fifth Era.

19th Century Disruptive Innovations

In 1913, at the peak of the Industrial Era, *Scientific American* conducted a survey with their readers asking them for a list of "the greatest innovations of our time." The readers of the magazine were encouraged to write essays, making the case for particular innovations that should be on the list. Then *Scientific American* extracted the full list of candidate innovations from those essays, created a short list of the most mentioned, and called for a vote of all readers of the magazine. This master list of the greatest innovations of the time was published in 1913.

Exhibit 3
The Greatest Innovations of Our Time – 1913

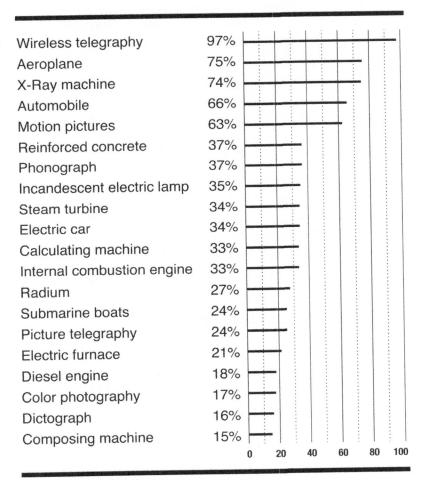

Source: *Scientific American*

In first place, we see wireless telegraphy was voted by 97% of *Scientific American* readers as being the top innovation. Next we see the airplane, X-ray machine, automobile, and so on.

The list is interesting in several ways. First, there was general agreement over which innovations were the most important in their time. The top five innovations were voted as the greatest by most voters, and then there is a significant drop-off as we reach the sixth innovation on the list: reinforced concrete. Secondly, many of the innovations are still central to our lives today—the airplane, X-ray machine, automobile, reinforced concrete, and incandescent electric lamp, to name just five. These innovations can be long-lived. Third, these innovations were very much characteristic of the Industrial Era at that time: they are almost all physical products that combine mechanical engineering with either fossil fuel or electrical energy sources, which is, of course, the defining essence of the Industrial Era itself.

The innovations on this list are disruptive, for sure, but they are not heralds of a disruption to the Industrial Era itself. *Scientific American* readers of 1913 were firmly in the middle of the Industrial Era—they were not living in a time of transition between eras.

20th Century Disruptive Innovations

Let us now look at the same question being asked by *Forbes Magazine* and The Wharton School in 2009. This time *Forbes* and Wharton asked readers to list "the top innovations of the prior 30 years" from 1979 through to 2009.

Exhibit 4

Forbes **List of the Top Innovations of the Prior 30 years – 2009**

1. Internet, broadband, www
2. PC/laptop computers
3. Mobile phones
4. E-mail
5. DNA testing and sequencing/human genome mapping
6. Magnetic Resonance Imaging (MRI)
7. Microprocessors
8. Fiber optics
9. Office software (spreadsheets, word processors)
10. Non-invasive laser/robotic surgery (laparoscopy)
11. Open-source software and services
12. Light-emitting diodes
13. Liquid crystal display (LCD)
14. GPS systems
15. Online shopping/e-commerce/auctions
16. Media file compression (jpeg, mpeg, mp3)
17. Microfinance
18. Photovoltaic solar energy
19. Large- scale wind turbines
20. Social networking via the Internet

Source: *Forbes Magazine* and The Wharton School, 2009

This list is very different from the list created in 1913. In 2009, some of the innovations are physical products just as they were in 1913—PC/laptop computers, mobile phones, MRI machines, and so on. But, more of the innovations are no longer physical at all— they are virtual innovations—the Internet, e-mail, various forms of software, and the activities the software enables, such as online shopping, social networking, and so on. Also, we have on this list the first of the major biotechnology breakthroughs: DNA testing and sequencing, and human genome mapping.

This list of the top innovations of the end of the twentieth century is shaped by two "mega" disruptive innovations—the Digital Revolution and the Biotechnology Revolution. The innovations mostly rest upon digital technologies. Many of them are virtual in nature, and in the case of breakthroughs in the life sciences, they focus on a better understanding and the engineering of life itself and of humankind.

The question to ask at this juncture is "Are these innovations of the last 30 years evolutionary and incremental within the context of the Industrial Era, or are they disruptive and so different from the innovations of the Industrial Era that they are heralds of a new era, the Fifth Era?"

We have concluded the latter, and expect that many of you are already convinced. But, for those who are unsure or who wish to argue that this is just another phase in the evolution of the Industrial Era, let's keep going and look at the next wave of disruptive innovations of the twenty-first century. In order to better explore the coming wave of disruptive innovations, let us first explore the two mega disruptive innovations of our time—the Digital Revolution and the Biotechnology Revolution.

The Digital Revolution

The Digital Revolution can be thought of as the time in which physical, mechanical innovations gave up their centrality in human life to virtual, digital innovations. Central among these—and the disruptive innovation that did the most to connect all human beings into one digitally connected entity—is the Internet. The Internet was invented by a handful of scientists as a resource for scientists. However, today, it has grown to become an essential instrument for more than four billion users worldwide.

Today, most industry sectors are being substantially transformed by this rapid and unprecedented expansion. For example, music, video, software, news, books, and even money markets are being reshaped because of the Internet. Human interactions have taken on a new nature as individuals use the Internet to gather information, educate themselves, go about their work, network socially, and entertain themselves and others. These changes are present and relevant in every region of the world, making the Internet a truly global and increasingly influential phenomenon.

Exhibit 5
Internet Penetration by Region

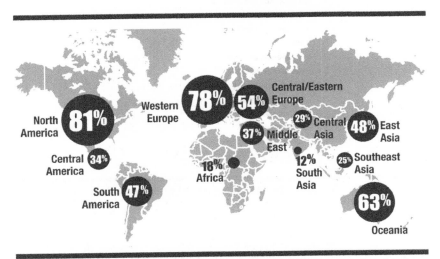

Sources: US Census Bureau, InternetWorldStats, CNNIC, Tencent, Facebook, ITU, CIAI, Fifth Era, LLC

While the process of change generated by the growth of the Internet and the emergence of new technologies has been swift and sweeping, it's far from complete. Substantial benefits are still to be captured. In this regard, the Digital Revolution is at the beginning rather than the end of its course. The Internet creates a tremendous amount of value for the global economy, substantially impacting GDP in most countries.

Exhibit 6

Internet Economy as a Percentage of 2016 GDP

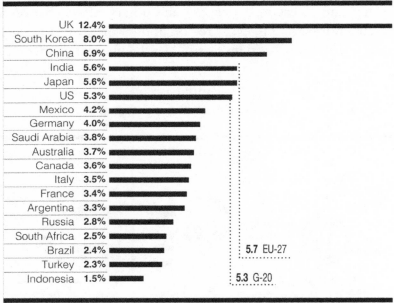

Sources: BCG Analysis; Economist Intelligence Unit; Organization for Economic Co-operation and Development (OECD), Fifth Era, LLC

In fact, the Internet contributes more to GDP than education and agriculture—two industries that are often highlighted in political decision-making.

Exhibit 7

Contribution of Selected Sectors to GDP

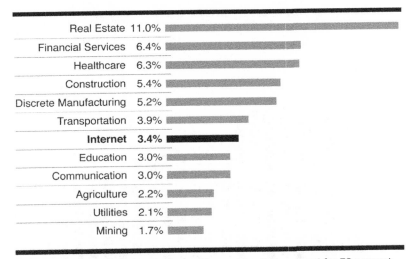

Real Estate	11.0%
Financial Services	6.4%
Healthcare	6.3%
Construction	5.4%
Discrete Manufacturing	5.2%
Transportation	3.9%
Internet	**3.4%**
Education	3.0%
Communication	3.0%
Agriculture	2.2%
Utilities	2.1%
Mining	1.7%

Note: Figures represent the following 13 countries that account for 70 percent of global GDP: Brazil, Canada, China, France, Germany, India, Italy, Japan, Russia, South Korea, Sweden, the United Kingdom, and the United States. Sources: Organization for Economic Co-operation and Development (OECD), Fifth Era, LLC

Fast-emerging technologies are expected to continue to drive the Internet and its innovation. We have already seen cloud services and the mobile Internet allowing everything everywhere to be accessed in terms of content and data, and paving the way for new services and applications that are, today, widespread and used by most of us. The proliferation of faster access through 4G and new high-speed computing technologies are especially important as they've also enabled this data access and supported new social-networking approaches.

Exhibit 8

Social Technologies Penetration by Country

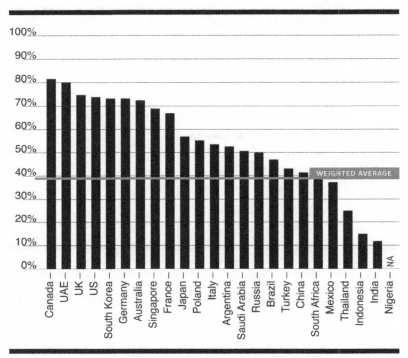

Sources: US Census Bureau, InternetWorldStats, CNNIC, Tencent, Facebook, ITU, CIA, Global Web Index, Fifth Era, LLC

The cloud, as well as more mobile connected devices, has also expanded such that the proportion of the global population covered by either mobile service or Internet access to at least 3G standards continues to expand rapidly. Today 3G is active in 181 countries and 4G in 63 countries, resulting in substantial increases in the penetration of the world's population by mobile devices.

Exhibit 9

Mobile Devices Penetration by Country

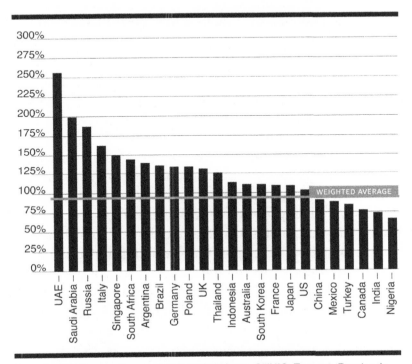

Sources: US Census Bureau, InternetWorldStats, CNNIC, Tencent, Facebook, ITU, CIA, Global Web Index, Fifth Era, LLC

Today it's inconceivable that we would be without the Internet, but just 30 years ago, it didn't even exist. This, as a disruptive influence, is unprecedented. In just a handful of years, we have gone from almost no Internet access for the majority of people, to upwards of four or five billion people incorporating it into their everyday life.

The Biotechnology Revolution

As explained in the first chapter of this book, for thousands of years, humankind used technology to engineer food production. During the Agrarian Era, we called this "domestication," and it was the process by which humans selected plants and animals, and emphasized in them the characteristics that they most valued and suppressed in them the characteristics that they no longer wanted to support. To a large extent, domestication was accomplished through multigenerational breeding of crops and animals in the direction that humans favored. Indeed, domestication was itself a disruptive innovation that took us into the Agrarian Era and has continued through today.

However, today's form of the domestication process—at the level of the gene—is fundamentally different from the processes of the past. The Biotechnology Revolution was ushered in by the fifth innovation listed on the 2009 *Forbes*/Wharton list: DNA testing and sequencing, and human genome mapping. These innovations allowed humans, for the first time, to look inside plants and animals, including human beings, and extend the process of domestication into engineering and evolving life itself.

In 2003 through 2005, my colleagues, Joan Chu and Nancy Michels, and I were invited by the State of California to develop a strategic action plan to ensure that the state's life sciences clusters remained at the forefront of the world's biotechnology revolution. To give some background, the term "cluster" refers to a geographic concentration of interconnected businesses, suppliers, and associated institutions in a particular field (Porter, 1998). Clusters are considered to increase the productivity with which companies can compete, nationally and globally. With that said, it makes sense the State of California wanted its life science clusters in the vanguard.

Working with the Monitor Group, a global strategy consulting firm, we developed a plan, which was widely accepted, that guided California's life sciences industry through a critical phase of development. The following synthesizes some of the findings of that work and continues to be true today, a decade later:

> Since these initial breakthroughs and their acceleration through the creation of the Human Genome Project (HGP) in the 1980s, the Biotechnology Revolution has seen the emergence of new sub-technologies and sub-specialties—entirely new areas of research unknown before. Proteomics, functional genomics, and bioinformatics are all examples of this HGP moving forward. This will continue to ratchet up as the demand for expertise in emerging areas of basic research are continued to ask for greater and new breakthroughs in the genome project. In the longer term, we are already beginning to see emerging technologies, such as gene therapy, stem cell research, and personalized medicine, also showing great promise for the continuing development of the life sciences industry globally.

> Today, every one of us relies upon the innovation breakthroughs of this Biotechnology Revolution. The medicines that we are prescribed when we are sick are, more often than not, the results of recent genomic insights that have led to the creation of new drugs and treatments. The food that we eat has, to a large extent, been influenced by the same Biotechnology Revolution. While controversial, genetically modified organisms are very much in the food chain today, and continuing research emphasizes the prospect that they will be even more so in the future. The animals that we rely upon for our sources of protein have, to a lesser extent, been impacted by the Biotechnology Revolution. While we give them biotechnology-engineered

foods and medicines, we have not to date engineered those animals to the extent that we now could—today's scientists know how to extend the process of domestication into engineering the genes of animals to better provide the characteristics that humans value. We have held back those scientists as society considers substantial questions about whether it supports this type of biotechnology-engineered animal livestock, but it's certainly something that we are already able to do—if we choose to do so. (Le Merle, M., Michels, N., & Chu, J., 2004)

The Biotechnology Revolution is the second major disruptive innovation of this transition period, and like the Digital Revolution, the resulting innovations stand in enormous contrast to the pre-existing medical technologies and innovations that were more common in the Industrial Era.

A Compounding of Innovations

Currently, the Digital Revolution and the Biotechnology Revolution are working together and compounding the impacts of each other. To date, this compounding has mostly moved in the direction of the Digital Revolution compounding the rate and impact of the Biotechnology Revolution. The former has allowed the ubiquitous availability of information, the speed and accessibility with which insights can be captured and shared, and the prospect of global collaboration between innovators and scientists to create new innovations together. We have seen remarkable rapid collaborative innovation to address global risks, such as severe acute respiratory syndrome (SARS) and Ebola, to name but two.

We are also seeing the flow of innovations beginning in the other direction as biotechnology (and chemistry and biology, more broadly defined) is beginning to be applied to new materials and approaches that may revolutionize computing and the Digital Revolution, just one example being the work on the organic chip and computer.

The Digital Revolution and the Biotechnology Revolution have already disrupted the global economy in dramatic ways, and they show the likelihood of even greater disruption in the future. But, they are only two of a number of emerging areas of disruptive innovation that we see transpiring today.

21st Century Disruptive Innovations

As we are writing this book in 2017, we see the emergence of a breadth of disruptive innovations more diverse than before, which offers the prospect of a plethora of specific inventions and breakthroughs. In 2016, we surveyed Keiretsu Forum (Sidebar 1: Keiretsu Forum and Keiretsu Capital), the world's largest angel investor network and the most active early-stage venture investor in the US, asking investors across North America to predict what the most promising areas of innovation are likely to be, using a survey question that Sharespost had asked of its investor group: "Regardless of time horizons, where do you see the greatest growth opportunities in the future?"

Exhibit 10 shows the resulting ranking of areas of disruptive innovations as predicted by these active angel investors.

Exhibit 10
Ranking of Disruptive Innovation Areas

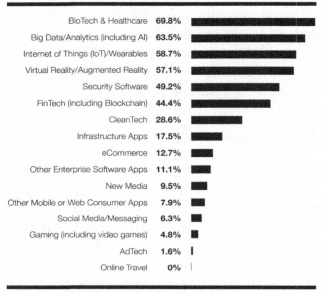

BioTech & Healthcare	69.8%	
Big Data/Analytics (including AI)	63.5%	
Internet of Things (IoT)/Wearables	58.7%	
Virtual Reality/Augmented Reality	57.1%	
Security Software	49.2%	
FinTech (including Blockchain)	44.4%	
CleanTech	28.6%	
Infrastructure Apps	17.5%	
eCommerce	12.7%	
Other Enterprise Software Apps	11.1%	
New Media	9.5%	
Other Mobile or Web Consumer Apps	7.9%	
Social Media/Messaging	6.3%	
Gaming (including video games)	4.8%	
AdTech	1.6%	
Online Travel	0%	

Sources: Keiretsu Capital, Fifth Era, LLC

Sidebar 1: Keiretsu Forum and Keiretsu Capital

We have been members and leaders of Keiretsu Forum and Keiretsu Capital for more than ten years, and many of the insights and opportunities that we describe in this book stem from that decade working with the other 2,500-plus angel investors that make up its membership.

Keiretsu Forum is a global investment community of accredited private equity angel investors, venture capitalists, and corporate/institutional investors. Keiretsu Forum was founded in the San Francisco East Bay in California in 2000 by Randy Williams. Keiretsu Forum is a worldwide network of capital, resources, and deal flow with 49 chapters on three continents. Keiretsu Forum members invest in high-quality, diverse investment opportunities. Keiretsu Forum and Keiretsu Capital (the exclusive worldwide fund partner of Keiretsu Forum) are ranked as the most active venture investors in the USA. The Keiretsu community is also strengthened through its involvement in social and charitable activities.

Exhibit 11

Most Active US Venture Investors, 2016

Most Active Investors Angel/Seed		Most Active Investors West Coast	
Firm	**Deals**	**Firm**	**Deals**
Keiretsu Forum	96	Keiretsu Forum	62
500 Startups	77	New Enterprise Associates	52
Innovation Works	25	Khosla Ventures	49
Y Combinator	24	Kleiner Perkins Caufield & Byers	42
Indian Angel Network	23	Andreessen Horowitz	41
Techstars	22	GV	37
Seedcamp	21	SV Angel	34
SV Angel	21	Y Combinator	34
Ben Franklin Technology Partners of Southeastern Pennsylvania	21	Accel Partners	33
SOSV	20	First Round Capital	32

Between 2006 and 2009, we were actively leading the San Francisco and North Bay chapters of Keiretsu Forum. Since 2007 we have launched and led Keiretsu Capital and the angel co-investment funds that it operates along with our fellow general partners Nathan McDonald and Randy Williams.

In order to understand these new areas of disruptive innovation and to illustrate how they are giving rise to new business opportunities, let's briefly describe the top seven of these areas of disruptive innovations. We will also give examples of emerging growth companies that we have backed through the Keiretsu Capital Angel Co-Investment Funds, or the Fifth Era Digital Future Fund, an early-stage fund investing in digital disruptions in the digital commerce, digital content, and FinTech areas. These examples might be helpful for readers who want case studies to better expand their understanding of these technologies; we do not claim these examples are necessarily predictions of the most important companies of the future.

Biotechnology and Healthcare

We consider the Biotechnology Revolution to be one of the most important disruptive forces of the last 30 years of innovation, and we expect the rate of innovation in biotechnology to only increase and accelerate. We expect to see substantial and disruptive innovations in healthcare, agriculture and animal husbandry, and in other areas, like forestry, fishing, and so on, on a scale that we have never seen before. We also expect to see new innovations where biotechnology is applied to the digital economy, including in areas like organic computing.

Not surprisingly, there are a number of companies that we are investing in that are pushing the forefront of this space. Just as three examples: Embera is developing the first medication that treats addiction by moderating activity in the stress response system to reduce the cravings and loss of control that drive addiction. LumiThera is a developmental stage medical device company at the forefront in the development of photobiomodulation treatment protocols for age-related macular degeneration. Savara Pharmaceuticals is a US-based emerging pharmaceutical development company that is focused on advancing a pipeline of novel inhalation therapies for the treatment of patients with rare pulmonary conditions.

The synergies between biotechnology and information technology are already fueling innovation in many areas from the more traditional pharmaceutical, digital health, and agricultural industries to emerging industries, such as industrial biotechnology. We are seeing greater convergence in the form of cross-industry technologies and applications, like bioinformatics and nanotechnology. A move toward personalized healthcare and personalized medicine will continue as scientists leverage genomic information, massive computing power, and big data analysis to gain a more fundamental understanding of diseases, biological processes, and proteins that affect various disease states. Therapies developed by life sciences firms are creating high levels of specialization for targeted patient populations, and, indeed, biotechnologies enable us to develop many targeted drugs with diagnostic tests to determine a priori whether a drug will be effective for a particular patient's genomic profile.

Big Data, Analytics, and Applications of Artificial Intelligence (AI)

The Internet has already enabled content to be accessed by almost anyone in the world in real time and on demand so long as permissions are made available by the owners of the content. Computing power breakthroughs, including parallel computing, allow us to analyze much more content much more rapidly. Investors expect that future innovations around big data analytics will allow us to gather insights from larger and larger data sets. These data sets are becoming so large that we rely upon the computer itself to make sense of them. These are the first applications of artificial intelligence (AI). AI algorithms allow researchers to gain better insights and to make better decisions from ever-larger data sets, leveraging ever-greater computing power.

One example of an emerging company that we have backed

that is operating in this space is Analyze. Analyze is an enterprise data, analytics, and software company based in Virginia. Analyze removes the friction between its clients and their data so that clients can surface actionable insights faster, leveraging their databases on 220 million US consumers and 360-plus unique data points on demographics, psychographic indicators, purchasing patterns, and more than 1 billion email addresses. Analyze is bringing AI and big data analytics to any consumer-facing company in any industry. A second example is DecisionNext, which is changing how companies do business in commodities-based industries. DecisionNext brings big data analytics to bear on commodities' sourcing and pricing decisions on behalf of its large corporate clients.

Of course, AI is not confined to helping make sense of data. AI holds the promise of making smart decisions too. In that regard, it opens up the possibility that machines can take over many decisions that are, today, made by humans. In so doing, and when combined with innovations in robotics, this also allows for a future in which smart machines take over many tasks that humans want to be released from, as well as undertake new tasks that we cannot imagine today. Some examples include early experiments in self-steering or even self-driving vehicles, smart exoskeletons that allow the physically handicapped to move again as fully able people do, similar experiments that allow amplified speed, power, and duration of human activities, and robots that can go places and do things that humans can't, such as enter and work in heavily radioactive environments, like Fukushima, or harsh environments, like Mars, or dangerous environments, like unexploded mine and bomb situations in Afghanistan and Iraq, and so on.

The applications are almost limitless, and at their heart are the emerging companies that work in big data, analytics, and AI. This is why investors score this area so highly in their ranking.

Wearables and the Internet of Things (IoT)

The first Internet that we have all experienced to date is one that primarily connects computers and mobile devices together and allows us, as individuals, to gather content and to interact with each other through those computing devices. The next major push in terms of the endpoints is to create sensors that allow other devices (beyond our computers and mobile devices) to also be connected to the Internet. These sensors allow, for example, a car or a refrigerator or a front doorbell to become a new connected endpoint of the Internet, and, in turn, this allows the Internet to extract information about the activities that these new endpoints are involved in. This "Internet of Things" (IoT) provides the promise that the devices we rely upon will one day be continuously monitored, enabling our service providers to take actions when they need to be fixed or replenished or replaced—though IoT holds the promise of much more than just these supporting activities.

Ooma is an IoT company that we work with at Fifth Era. Today, Ooma is a public company that is committed to transforming the landscape of home phone service and enabling the future of the digital home. At the center of their current offering is Ooma Office, an enterprise-level phone service for small businesses and Ooma Telo, a highly sophisticated computer that when connected to Ooma's cloud-based smart platform, delivers free calling with extremely high quality, advanced features, and connected services such that it turns any phone into a smartphone for your home.

Once IoT hubs, like Ooma, become established in offices and homes, they provide the potential to allow other less smart devices to be connected to the Internet, enabling the vision of a world of connected devices. Of course, the IoT is not just a home- or consumer-focused area of disruptive innovations. IoT is being extended into every industry and to every imaginable endpoint device. Examples include dispensing machines that know which sodas or snacks are most likely to need replenishment or what advertisements to show as users approach them at various times of the day. Another example is buildings that monitor who is in each room and whether heat, light, and sound should be adjusted, based upon occupancy and motion. There are technologies being deployed that monitor what parking spaces are used and provide the data to applications so that drivers don't endlessly circle, hoping to find a vacant space, but are, instead, directed in real time to slots as they open and close. And so on.

Wearables is the extension of this thought process to the clothes and the accessories that we carry with us every day. Over the last couple of decades, most of us have supplemented our attire with a smart computing device that we used to think of as a phone, which, today, we think of as a powerful computer in a phone format: a smartphone. Wearables innovations take us to the next stage, potentially engineering the computing device and integrating it into accessories that we wear or even stitching it virtually throughout the clothes that we put on our bodies. Just as the IoT greatly expands the collection of and use of content from each of its endpoint devices, so the wearables movement could do the same for the wardrobes that we wear. One very novel company we have invested in is Textile-Based Delivery (Texdel), which has invented four patent-pending "platform" technologies that enable the secure and controlled delivery of "active" ingredients to a target location over a long period of time and through hundreds of laundering cycles. This means that apparel can be engineered to deliver vitamins, cosmetics, and even drugs to wearers over time. Examples might include driving gloves with caffeine in them, swimming costumes with built-in sunscreen, or even underwear that delivers needed vitamins.

Virtual Reality and Augmented Reality

In 1998, we were asked by the City of San Francisco and the Bay Area Council to create a strategic plan for the "multimedia industry" of the city to ensure that California would become the global leader in multimedia to add to its traditional leadership in the film industry by way of the Hollywood film cluster. Central to that strategy for San Francisco was the creation of a cluster that would combine digital technologies and the Internet with video game content creation to form a new digital entertainment industry.

Over the last two decades since we created that plan, San Francisco and the Bay Area have become the world's leading digital entertainment cluster, and we have seen innovations in the ways that we access content and visualize and interact with information globally. In many industries, including entertainment, education, and military applications, we have sought to improve access devices that strive for even higher resolution and greater immersiveness through richer viewing experiences and better sound.

The next step in this continuing innovation around our access devices is expected to be in the areas of virtual reality (VR) and augmented reality (AR). Virtual reality enables participants to step into the content and be a part of it, whereas augmented reality allows participants to layer information on top of real-world images that they may be experiencing. Billions of dollars are being invested in both of these areas as well as in mixed-reality solutions that incorporate aspects of both virtual and augmented reality. The gains in experience by increasing the immersiveness of our devices and allowing us to step into the data and live the data and the content are expected to be transformational in nature.

An application of these technologies that is already gaining widespread acceptance is in digital entertainment. Here video game makers and film producers are allowing users to experience

360-degree videos where they can rotate their viewing position to see the content in 3D rather than 2D and with a 360-degree field of view. The same video game makers are also applying virtual reality to computer-generated content. The opportunity is even greater here because the content is being rendered by a computer, and the viewer can not only step into the content and view it from different directions, but can actually interact with the computer-generated assets and environments: picking up objects, physically interacting with characters, and shaping the experience. Unlike 360-degree video, which captures an image but can't then change that image, CGI VR (computer generated imagery virtual reality) allows the content to be dynamically modified as the viewer interacts with it.

An example of a very innovative company we have backed that is pushing the frontier of CGI VR in entertainment is Waygate/VRTV. Here, a team of industry veterans from Telltale Games and Zynga has created a platform that delivers fully interactive VR experiences through real-time, native 3D rendering—not video. (Note: "Native" means that the software was developed for a device and its own operating system—rather than being developed for some other operating system.) Their platform allows all of the content to be streamed in real time from the cloud directly to the user's device. This is a breakthrough when compared to the very long download times that most large VR files require, and because the content is rendered natively on each device, there is no latency, pauses, or stuttering. This means the user experience is immersive and immediate.

Of course, VR and AR are not confined to entertainment applications. We are seeing emerging companies apply these technologies across a breadth of industries: VR to help surgeons operate on patients remotely; VR that allows potential buyers in China to walk through apartments in Los Angeles and New York, admiring the views from each window, opening each door, and seeing how the surfaces will be finished; and AR applications that allow industrial equipment technicians to have instruction manuals and guides to be projected into their lines of sight as they open up industrial machinery in factories and determine how best to fix it. These are just a handful of examples from a plethora that are now being envisioned and created.

Security Software

The Internet is evolving as we continue to add increased computer power, more powerful high-speed networks, more endpoint devices, and ever-increasing amounts of content. But, the Internet is also open to less positive changes as hostile players choose to attack, for whatever purpose, the Internet and its activity. Cybersecurity and the rise of very responsive security hardware and software are the next areas that investors expect to be very fruitful for new innovations. Security software also extends into the physical world. As we see the extension of new security networks into the physical world through, for example, video surveillance systems at our homes, places of work, and public places, security software needs to become ever more effective and reliable.

Viakoo is an example of another start-up we have backed that provides operational intelligence for physical security systems. Leveraging purpose-built technology, Viakoo quickly and automatically detects physical security system failures, diagnoses the problem, and then alerts users, telling them how to fix it. The company, based in Mountain View, California, is operating at the very frontier of operational intelligence in which real-time dynamic business analytics are delivering visibility and insights into data, streaming events and business operations, and, in this case, improving the integrity and effectiveness of video-based security networks.

As we will show in the next chapter, the risks inherent in cybersecurity form a potential wildcard that could interrupt the very thesis of this story: that we are entering a Fifth Era of human existence. We will return to this theme in Chapter 3, but suffice to say that the capital that will flow to security software and the arms race that is occurring in this space provide some of the rationales for why early-stage investors view this as likely to be one of the top five value-creation opportunities of our time.

FinTech and Blockchain

The financial industry has always been a highly digital industry since money has evolved over time to essentially be a digital, rather than a physical, medium in most applications in most parts of the world. Since money became digital so early, computers became essential to the financial industry and processes globally, and we saw the growth of an industry focused on technologies that support these very large industries (FinTech). Continuing breakthroughs are expected as new technologies are applied to the legacy financial infrastructure that was created at the end of the twentieth century. Foremost amongst these is the distributed ledger or blockchain, which holds the promise of allowing much more powerful real-time confirmation of trades and the people who are trading with each other. Early applications suggest that blockchain can not only improve the productivity of financial activities but also eliminate the need to maintain large, complex, and burdensome legacy infrastructure.

We are partnered with Blockchain Capital Partners, which is among the most active investors in early-stage companies that are utilizing the new innovations in the blockchain arena. We are continually impressed by how teams of entrepreneurs are finding real-world applications for blockchain both in financial services and also in other industries where transactions need to be validated in real time and where information needs to be secure and transactions recorded for future review. We are also seeing industry incumbents across industries, from banking and insurance, to healthcare and real estate, see valuable applications in their industries.

FinTech is, of course, much broader than just blockchain. Broadly defined, the financial industries, like banking, investments, insurance, trading, and so on, compose perhaps the largest industry on the face of the earth. While they were "digitized" very early, that also indicates the reality that their infrastructure is "first generation." Most large financial industry companies have aging legacy computing infrastructure that needs to be brought into the new world of cloud, big data, AI, and so on. And perhaps even more importantly, the financial industry is itself powering every other industry because it enables the workings of global commerce and transactions. We have backed two FinTech companies, ApplePie Capital and Sindeo, that focus on these convergence spaces. ApplePie Capital is a peer-to-peer lending platform that allows any franchisee to get financing while Sindeo brings a more digital-enabled platform to help real-estate investors get their financing, beginning with homebuyers.

So, FinTech is seen as a top area of future growth and wealth creation both because it is mission-critical to one of the world's largest industries and because it is enabling new transaction and payment systems to every other industry, including all of those new industries being unleashed by the Digital Revolution.

Clean Technologies

In the overview of the Industrial Era, we described the three phases through which the Industrial Era moved, powered first by coal and steam, then by other fossil fuels, and most recently by electricity. Clean technologies hold the promise that humans will be able to find even more powerful and more sustainable approaches to generating the energy sources that they need to power all of the innovations described in this section and that will come. Whether it be areas that we've explored for centuries—wind, water, and solar power—or new and emerging areas, such as fuel cells and nuclear fission and fusion, increasing investment and entrepreneurial energy is being focused on finding clean technologies for the Fifth Era. In addition, clean technologies include those innovations that help maintain the cleanliness of our air, water, and Earth for future generations.

We have made a number of investments in this space, including our support of The Clean Fund, based in California, which is the leading provider of long-term financing for energy efficiency, water conservation, renewable energy, and seismic improvements for commercial, multifamily, and other nonresidential properties in the US. For almost a decade, we have worked closely with Shanshan Group of China, the world's leading provider of lithium carbonate and a significant player in other clean energy sources. And, with Keiretsu Capital, we have invested in companies, such as Indow, which creates window inserts that reduce energy costs, Phytonix, which is an industrial biotechnology company, producing sustainable chemicals directly from carbon dioxide, and has the objective to be the global leader in bio-safe, direct solar chemicals and fuel production, utilizing carbon dioxide as the sole feedstock and energy from the sun, and SafeH2O, which is a water biodetection company, providing rapid pathogen test systems and data services, assisting water providers and servicers in reducing illness, and assuring sustainability of water systems.

Clean technologies are critical to the long-term sustainable development of the earth and will be needed in the future as fossil fuels eventually become scarce and their disadvantages too burdensome. Given the almost limitless sources of energy from the sun, water and wind, most investors see future wealth generation opportunities in these areas. Additionally, investors know that a lot of money will be made cleaning up the negative impacts of Industrial Era energy sources during the time of transition to the Fifth Era.

And All the Others Too

The top seven areas of disruptive innovation detailed above show just how ubiquitous innovation will be over the next few decades as the Digital and Biotechnology Revolutions continue to transform our age.

Investors are also excited by other areas of disruptive innovation:

Continuing *advances in infrastructure applications* that enable every business to be in the cloud, connected and effective on other people's platforms, like Amazon web services, Google Enterprise and Applications, and Microsoft Azure, to name just three, is one such area.

Opportunities in the continuing *evolution of electronic commerce*, which was one of the hallmarks of the initial expansion of the Internet, allowing us to find, purchase, and receive goods and services electronically, whereas before we would have relied upon physical retailing, in most cases. The next wave of e-commerce is pushing the envelope by doing an even better job of predicting our individual needs, surfacing alternatives that are personalized to our own circumstances, and allowing us to access the products and services we want, wherever we want them, at the time that we most need them. This next phase of electronic commerce is also expected to be much more immersive, leveraging some of the breakthroughs we've already described in areas, such as big data analytics and AI, in VR and AR, relying upon the breakthroughs of the blockchain and financial technologies, and potentially also incorporating IoT and wearables breakthroughs. This compounding of innovations is a theme that is important and one that we'll return to later.

We continue to see more and more powerful *endpoint devices* as described already. As social animals, it's no surprise that one of the major uses to which we apply this real-time connected capability is to communicate with other human beings. New breakthroughs in social media are allowing us to do that in more and more rich and robust ways. And, we still need to connect another one or two billion people into that conversation.

In the past, we've entertained ourselves through a variety of media, including books, newspapers, films, radio, TV, music, and so on. Most of these entertainment formats are broadcast formats. Conversely, nowadays most people seek to interact during their entertainment, and many people want to be a part of creating the entertainment experience. People's desire for more interactivity and the ability to express their own creativity is something that new technologies are beginning to enable at an ever-increasing rate. *Immersive, interactive entertainment* holds the promise that we will all become creators of entertainment experiences and fully immersed in the experiences that we create with others.

In the travel industry, we see two dimensions of rapid expansion and growth. The first is that a greater percentage of the population of the world is beginning to travel, and we're seeing hundreds of millions of people, including in China and India, getting to a level of affluence where travel for entertainment is an option for them. Secondly, we're also seeing the expansion of virtual travel where people use some of the technologies we've already described to have virtual travel experiences, enabling them to go places where, in practice, they would never be able to travel physically. This part of the *digital travel experience* is expected both to be a very substantial growth opportunity and also a potential disruptor of traditional modes of tourism and travel.

We have been placing our own bets in all of these areas too—Acceleration Systems and Curb in infrastructure applications, 1World Online, Perkville, and Social Standards in e-commerce and social, Telltale Games, Soundwave, and Spotify in digital entertainment, and LesConcierges/John Paul in the new travel industry—just to mention a handful.

Do These Innovations Make a Positive Difference?

Disruptive innovations bring with them disruption and change—by definition. In most cases, an established business or activity is disrupted while a new business or activity is created. At this point in our story, it makes sense to ask: Is this, on balance, positive for the world and for humankind? On balance, do disruptive innovations, like we are seeing today, move us forward? Do they create more than they destroy?

The answer is—yes they do, when viewed from an economic perspective. A recent study by researchers from our alma mater, Stanford University, confirms this. Researchers Kogan, Papanikolaou, Seru, and Stoffman (2016) just completed an analysis of all patents issued to US firms between 1926 and 2010. They assessed the degree to which these patents created scientific and economic value and creative destruction. Across all three metrics, they were able to show high levels of positive gain associated with the patent activity. From an economic perspective, disruptive innovations make a positive difference.

Societally, are these disruptive innovations also positive? This is a harder question to answer because it requires us to know what the future of society will look like and then make a personal judgment as to whether we value that future higher than the current society(ies) in which we live today. We don't have the answer to this second question. For us, we believe that the value that disruptive innovations bring by solving society's most pressing problems has never been greater—whether we are talking about the need for clean air, water, and earth, more food for everyone, better healthcare and longer life, improved working conditions, more availability of knowledge and education, sustainable sources of clean energy, less congestion in our cities, and so forth. We are sure that the technologies and approaches that got 7.5 billion of us to this point will not be able to solve the challenging issues of today, let alone those that will surface in the future. Only new innovations will make sure that our children, and their children, live in a world where these and many other issues have been solved.

Never has it been so true that necessity must be the mother of invention—the greatest challenges of our time demand innovative solutions.

By now, you have reviewed examples of the types of disruptive innovations that are coming, or perhaps you have your own view—and as Mahatma Gandhi said, "You must be the change you wish to see in the world."

A World of Opportunities Ahead

To conclude this chapter, the world is seeing incredible opportunities being created by a breadth of disruptive innovations. And, there is much more coming. We don't know what the list of top innovations will be when a future survey is taken in 2116. What we do know is that it will be profoundly shaped by the Digital Revolution, the Biotechnology Revolution, and the compounding of the two. We also know that many of the long list of disruptive innovations that inventors are currently working on and that we have just described will have been deployed globally and across industries, transforming our lives and improving the condition of humankind.

Gordon Moore, co-founder of Intel, the world's leading semiconductor company, observed in 1965 that "the number of transistors per square inch on integrated circuits has doubled every year since the integrated circuit was invented." He went on to predict that this trend would continue for the foreseeable future. We know this as Moore's law.

If we, Matthew Le Merle and Alison Davis, were to seek to create a similar law for the Fifth Era, it would be that "the compounding of digital with biotechnology innovations will accelerate disruptive change at a rate that humankind has never experienced before. We can only begin to imagine just how different the Fifth Era will be."

Because these innovations are so very different from the incremental changes that occurred within the phases of the Industrial Era, we feel absolutely confident that they, in total, represent the shift to a new era—and that we are living in a time of transition.

In the next chapter, we will explore just how different living in the Fifth Era might be.

Chapter 3
Glimpses of the Fifth Era

Change is the law of life. And those who look only to the past or present are certain to miss the future.

—*John F. Kennedy*

Another lens through which to view this Fifth Era is to explore specific aspects of human beings and see if these innovations would change us dramatically or not. If not, then perhaps we are just evolving the Industrial Era into a new phase. If it is likely that how we behave and interact as human beings are likely to change dramatically, then we are certainly in a new era.

Let's explore how different the future might be and the magnitude of the disruption and wealth creation that is likely to occur.

Human Activities Built upon Underlying Assumptions

In each era, humans conduct their activities within the modus operandi of the era. They live and work and play within an "era mindset," a set of underlying assumptions, methods, and beliefs that are so established that it shapes their view as to what is possible and, as a result, what can be. But, when disruptive innovations attack that mindset and those underlying assumptions, we tend to see inertia continue the old ways of being longer than is strictly necessary. It takes a while for disruptive innovations to enable new ways of being and for the old order to be displaced. This is why transitions between eras are not clean and linear, but rather messy, overlapping, and chaotic, and it is only when old ways of being have been displaced that we move into the next era.

Let's look at three central aspects of our lives in the Industrial Era and see if they are still likely to be the way that they have been. Are the underlying assumptions on which they were designed still valid? Or, have disruptive innovations knocked out the Industrial Era rationale for their design, providing the preconditions for new approaches?

Generation C

In order to examine areas of our lives, we should first introduce the notion of Generation C (see Sidebar 2). This is the portion of the world's population that was born after 1990 and has only known a connected existence. They are unaware of a time before the Internet and don't understand many of the assumptions that shape the mindsets of older people and rule their decisions and actions. Yes, we have heard of Generations X, Y, and Z, but we see them all as vertical slices through a more fundamental transition—from our generation, generally born before 1990, and which grew up in an unconnected world—to a new generation, Generation C, that is growing up always connected into the whole.

In 2010, we were part of a team at Booz & Company, the consulting firm (now a part of PWC) that surveyed this "connected generation" around the world. We found that this Generation C simply does not think in the same way as prior generations. They are ready for new approaches that the next era is ready to unleash.

Sidebar 2: Generation C

By the year 2020, an entire generation will have grown up in a primarily digital world. Computers, the Internet, mobile phones, texting, social networking—all are second nature to them. And their familiarity with technology, reliance on mobile communications, and desire to remain in contact with large networks of family members, friends, business contacts, and others will transform how we work and how we consume. This is the demographic group we call Generation C—the C stands for connect, communicate, change.

What Is Generation C?

What is Generation C? They are realists, they are materialists. They are culturally liberal, if not politically progressive. They are upwardly mobile, yet they live with their parents longer than others ever did. Many of their social interactions take place on the Internet, where they feel free to express their opinions and attitudes. They've grown up under the influence of Harry Potter, Barack Obama, and iEverything—iPods, iTunes, iPhones. Technology is so intimately woven into their lives that the concept of "early adopter" is essentially meaningless.

They are Generation C—connected, communicating, content-centric, computerized, community-oriented, always clicking. As a rule, they were born after 1990 and lived their adolescent years after 2000. In the developed world, Generation C encompasses everyone in this age group; in the BRIC countries, they are primarily urban and suburban. By 2020, they will make up 40 percent of the population in the US, Europe, and the BRIC countries, and 10 percent in the rest of the world—and by then, they will constitute the largest group of consumers worldwide.

Having owned digital devices all their lives, they are intimately familiar with them and use them as much as six hours a day. They all have mobile phones and constantly send text messages. More than

95 percent of them have computers, and more than half use instant messaging to communicate, have Facebook pages, and watch videos on YouTube.

Consider the typical Gen C "digital native" in 2020—Colin is a 20-year-old computer science student in London, where he lives with two other students on the equivalent of about €600 a month. He enjoys backpacking, sports, music, and gaming. He has a primary digital device (PDD) that keeps him connected 24 hours a day—at home, in transit, and at school. He uses it to download and record music, video, and other content, and to keep in touch with his family, friends, and an ever-widening circle of acquaintances. His apartment is equipped with the latest wireless home technology with download speeds mandated by the government.

Colin's parents are divorced, and he has one sister. He is close to his family, but his actual physical contact with them is limited. Instead, he prefers to stay in touch through his PDD, which allows him to communicate simultaneously through multiple channels—voice, text, video, data—either to them individually or to all of them at once. His parents would prefer that he visit more often, of course, but they are finally beginning to get used to being a part of his digital life. Still, sometimes Colin feels he is too digitally connected; for example, a recent surprise visit to his mother was ruined because she knew he was in town—he had forgotten to disable the location feature on his PDD. Colin's social life is also mediated through his PDD. He can always find out the location of his friends, even what they are doing, and communicate with them instantly.

Much of Colin's experience at school is mediated by his PDD. He can attend lectures, browse reading material, do research, compare notes with classmates, and even take exams—all from the comfort of his apartment. When he does go to campus, his PDD automatically connects to the school's network and downloads relevant content, notices, even bills for fees, and he can authorize their payment later, at his leisure. His PDD does most of the work for him when he's shopping too. Though he prefers to shop online, when he does visit a store, the PDD automatically connects to the store's network, guiding him through product choices, offering peer reviews, and automatically checking out and paying for items he purchases.

Colin's real passion is traveling, preferably with a backpack. On a recent trip to Australia, his PDD kept him occupied throughout the long plane ride, then helped him through customs by automatically connecting to the Australian government's network. Colin used the PDD to pinpoint the location of Australian friends he was going to travel with (he had met them on the Internet). Once they met up, they used their PDDs to plan their route, a relatively easy task, given that with the entire world was already modeled in 3D they could see every twist and turn on their path. No surprises there!

Exhibit 12

A Day in the Life of a Generation C Consumer, 2020

20-Year Old Leo Q's Day: April 12, 2020

07:00 Reading news on personal digital device (PDD)
  – Twittering plans for the day

07:30 Checking e-health tool: first symptoms of sinusitis;
  message on PDD for doctor's appointment

08:00 E-vote on "ban of motor vehicles in Berlin governmental area"
  referendum via "digital ID"

9:00 Interactive video e-learning session with professor

11:30 Short video chat with grandmother - Sharing tasks via cloud project tool

13:30 Navigation-supported drive to doctor
  – Real-time smart routing to avoid traffic congestion

15:30 Unlock clinical record for doctor; medication sent to home

18:00 Shopping downtown: online price check with PDD,
  friend recommendations on intended couch purchase
  – Shopping tour picture sharing on profile

19:30 Downtown walk: friends join for location-based 30% discount promotion
  for dinner at small restaurant
  – M-payment for food

22:30 Retiring: e-book and simultaneous streamed video
  – Automated reminder via PDD to take sinusitis medication before 23:00

Sources: Fredrich R., Le Merle M., Peterson M., Koster A. (2010)

We will now look at aspects of how we make friends, how we learn, and how we work, as three examples to make the general case that all human activities are being impacted by the innovations that surround us today.

How We Make Friends

Making friends is one of the most important human activities in that it is a foundation for all social endeavors.

How Many Friends Do You Have?
We asked members of our generation and members of Generation C a handful of questions. First, we asked, "How many friends do you have?" Members of our generation, generally born before 1990, typically say 100, more or less. Generation C typically says more—maybe 250 or 300.

How Many Have You Met?
We then asked both groups, "How many of your friends have you met in person?" Our generation laughs, replying, "All of them, of course." Generation C responds with a perfectly straight face, "Most of them I haven't met." They don't see this as an odd question at all. Why do you need to physically meet people to be friends with them? "What a strange concept," they seem to say.

How Do You Define a Friend?
Then we asked both groups, "What makes a friend a friend?" Both generations answer very similarly: a friend is someone you know, trust, share confidences with in both directions, use as a sounding board, appreciate having the support of, etc. Both our generation and Generation C have the same definition of what a friend is.

What Do You Do With Your Friends?
Next, we explored with both groups what they do with their

friends. How often do they interact? When was the last interaction? What confidences have they shared recently? What confidences have their friends shared? And so on.

And we find, consistently, that Generation C is living up to the definition of friendship with their friends while our generation is not. Indeed, by the very definition of friendship given by those in our generation, our generation has even fewer friends than they declared at the outset while in many cases Generation C has more.

Whose Friends Are More Real?

So, who has more friends and whose friends are more real? The answer is Generation C. Why? Because they have released themselves from the Industrial Era mindset that friendships need to be physically based and because they have embraced digital innovations that allow them to build virtual friendships with people they have not yet met in person.

Why is this such a dramatic example? Because, if society can build deep and enduring, trust-based relationships so easily with people that have never been met in person and if those friendships can be made to endure and can be multiplied and maintained in ever-larger numbers, this in turn greatly expands the scope and scale of so many other human activities in connected, real-time, and continuous ways. This impacts learning, socializing, entertaining, working, and every other human activity.

How We Learn

Let's consider a second part of our lives that has similarly been transformed by the Digital Revolution. Learning is the work of a lifetime, and humans learn all the time. However, to illustrate the most important themes of this chapter, let's focus on one particular component of learning—higher education and the role of universities and colleges of higher learning. We've made this the focus because it is the pinnacle of our organized learning process today. We can expect insights we derive from this focus to ripple back down into the school system towards our earliest days, as well as forward into corporate and continuing learning systems.

The University in the Industrial Era

The university, including colleges of higher education, is a globally accepted element of how we are educated within the Industrial Era. While some early universities began to appear in the Agrarian Era and many more were formed in the Mercantile Era, the university became universally accepted as the principal approach to higher education during the Industrial Era, displacing private tutoring, the apprentice system, and self-learning.

In the fall of 2016, some 20.5 million students were in attendance at American colleges and universities, constituting an increase of about 5.2 million since fall 2000. About 7.2 million students will attend two-year institutions, and 13.3 million will attend four-year institutions. Some 17.5 million students enrolled in undergraduate programs, and about 3.0 million enrolled in post-baccalaureate programs (National Center for Education Statistics, 2016).

Why?

University: The Underlying Assumptions

During the Agrarian Era, knowledge was in short supply. Those who had it were rare. Most people did not read or write, and most people were not formally educated. A few people were exceptions to that rule. They sought out knowledge, wrote it down—by hand—and were willing to share it with like-minded people.

Because they were so few, they clustered together, around libraries that hosted the carefully hand-written scrolls and early books that documented their knowledge, or they met around a tree, in a courtyard, or in a chamber and talked to each other.

If you wanted to learn, you had no choice but to travel to these few locations. Most people were not wealthy enough to be able to afford the trip or the time off from farming the land. Those few that did, arrived in the place of knowledge, and listened and learned. Perhaps they stayed or perhaps they returned home.

After the invention of the printing press, more knowledge could be captured and shared, but even then the learned teachers were few in number. And they still preferred to cluster. They remained in centers of knowledge and agreed to teach in those places.

Over time these locations became more established, more formalized, more populated. And the role of teacher and student became more accepted and established.

Over time the university was born.

The University: Disrupting the Underlying Assumptions

Now let's look again at each of those underlying assumptions through the most recent lens of this time of transition. As we look, we'll pose the question, "Is this underlying assumption still true?"

Knowledge is in short supply—is this assumption still true? No. Today most knowledge is captured and instantly available to anyone anywhere. This is one of the great benefits of the Internet and those who have made the world's knowledge available to everyone.

Those who have this knowledge are rare—is this assumption still true? No. Today indexes and searches allow anyone to explore the available knowledge and find what they are seeking. Additionally, most knowledge has been captured and stored online.

Most people do not read or write—is this assumption still true? No. Over the last part of the Industrial Era, almost everyone around the world has become literate: the World Factbook estimates 82% of the world's population is now in this group (Central

Intelligence Agency, 2016).

Knowledge has to be concentrated into libraries—is this assumption still true? No. Knowledge can be everywhere in the cloud and accessible everywhere through the Internet.

People need to meet physically to learn—is this assumption still true? Maybe. While remote electronic learning can be effective, especially for the connected generation that views this as their preferred learning mode (see Sidebar 2: Generation C), for many, and especially for the teachers who were brought up in the old model, physical teaching and tutoring still has its merits.

Most people are not wealthy enough to attend university—is this assumption still true? No. Once the costs of the physical university and attending it in person are removed from the equation, the cost of accessing the knowledge, having it taught, and learning it becomes trivial. It is the physical model of the university, with the need for unleveraged teachers and expensive buildings and grounds, that drives the cost of that model.

In short, the Digital Revolution has undermined every underlying assumption for why we have universities as centers of learning. Of course, exceptions still exist. For example, certain laboratory or research activities still need to be performed in physical locations. Even here we are creating virtual simulations that may undermine these exceptions.

So, why do we still have universities?

Because teachers and parents were themselves taught in the Industrial Era model and have not become comfortable with the Fifth Era innovations and because of inertia and the sizable legacy infrastructure of buildings, classrooms, libraries, residence halls, athletic facilities, and so on.

Does this inertia mean that we will never see virtual learning of high education knowledge?

We don't think so. The disruptive innovations of the Digital Revolution have already enabled a transition of higher education from the Industrial Era model to a new Fifth Era model of virtual learning. But, it will take time for new ways to displace old ways. Maybe decades, maybe centuries. Maybe faster. Notwithstanding this uncertainty over the transition timing, there is sure to be a significant wealth-creation opportunity for those who lead in the creation and deployment of the new Fifth Era learning models.

How Fast Could This Change?

In parts of the world where physical institutions of higher learning have already been built, there is more resistance to changing the underlying model. In parts of the world where physical institutions of higher learning have not been built, the case for change gets more notice and support.

Consider China. China's population was more than 1.35 billion in 2016. An increasing proportion of the Chinese population is "middle class" and expect access to good education for their children. By 2022 McKinsey and Company expects 75% of Chinese to be middle class (Barton, Chen, & Jin, 2013). With a large and growing inland Chinese middle class (McKinsey estimates they will represent 39% of the total Chinese middle class by 2022) located in the inland cities where there is limited access to the best learning, what should the Chinese do? Build vast numbers of physical universities across the country? Allow their students to travel to the coastal cities? Ship them to American universities? Perhaps, all of the above?

Given the disruptive innovations of recent years, why not promote virtual learning and allow students to remain where they are, join virtual classrooms, and get educated according to a new model? This is the thrust of the very significant rise in remote technology-enabled learning across China. We have recently joint ventured with Talkweb, one of China's leading technology-enabled learning platforms and their growth is quite remarkable.

Who Will Capture the Opportunity?

Who will win? Again, it is not clear. A priori there is value in the existing university brands and teaching excellence. If branded institutions, like our alma maters Cambridge, Harvard, Oxford, and Stanford, embrace the new world and work hard to solve the remaining challenges, then surely they have an advantage since they have brands, reputations, and a great number of other assets developed over hundreds of years and not shared by start-ups. Why would upstarts and start-ups be better positioned?

Why do we highlight higher education and learning? Because, if we can move to approaches in which all of the world's 7.5 billion people (and one day many more) can gain the full benefits of human knowledge through scalable, inexpensive, and universally available learning platforms, then surely we have an opportunity to unleash the full capability of so many more billions of people than we are able to today.

Imagine what humankind could achieve if 10 or 100 or 1,000 times as many people were able to bring their full potentials to bear on our most pressing issues through the power of virtual learning, collaboration, and problem-solving platforms.

How We Work

Here is one last example to illustrate our thesis: that the Industrial Era's underlying assumptions have been undermined by new disruptive technologies, which, in turn, are opening up enormous new opportunities for entrepreneurs and the people that back them.

Work - Our Invention

Work is the greatest invention of the Industrial Era. In the Hunter-Gatherer Era, it was not even a notion. You did what you needed to do to sustain yourself, and the rest of your time was for you. But, in the Industrial Era the rise of the corporate model of business and everything that went with it established almost universal beliefs and expectations about "work," assumptions that we live with today, that rule our lives and shape many of our notions of what a life even looks like.

How Does Our Generation Define Work?

When asked, our generation (people generally born before 1990) defers to a definition of work that is the result of how things were done in the Industrial Era. We talk about work needing a workplace. Work is something that has defined hours—typically Monday to Friday from 9 am until 5 pm. There are employers who are mostly large corporations, and there are bosses in a hierarchical pyramid who direct our work and whom we report to. We expect to work in the same job for many years—sometimes for a lifetime. And when we eventually retire, we expect to be supported either by the companies we worked a lifetime for or by government-created support programs funded by those companies and by taxes.

How Does Generation C Define It?

Then ask Generation C how they define work. They have very different answers. Work is something you do to make the money to pursue your other interests. It is something you do when you want to. Sometimes you may have one employer, sometimes you have several, and sometimes you do work on your own. You expect not only to have many jobs over your lifetime, but also at any given time. It is not "moonlighting," it is your choice to do as many jobs as you want. Maybe you take time off from one job to do another. Maybe you do a second job at lunchtime or on your computer during downtime in your first job. Employers, bosses, defined hours, and defined places of work are notions recognized by Generation C, but the logic for them is often not understood. "Why should we go to an office if we can do work more effectively remotely?" "We get much more done on our computer, so why do our older work colleagues insist on burning up most of the day in conference room meetings?" "Let's just agree on the work that needs doing on a shared online document and get it done." "I am at my best when I do what I need to do in the order that makes sense to me." "I don't understand why others prescribe my work style to me when they don't understand how my generation and I work?"

Who Is right?

Of course, both are right. Because they are each adhering to the respective beliefs of their times. But, Generation C is right for the future. Because the future is theirs and work will change to fit the preferences and expectations of the future generation, we should expect that they will change the working approaches and practices that no longer make sense in a digitally enabled world. But, the transition time may be long. Concepts, like "the sharing economy," "services on-demand," "virtual workplaces," and so on, are fundamentally important because they are the first experiments in creating new working practices that better fit people's future new realities. While any one of these experiments may fail, they are still evidence of a growing gap between how we work in the final stages of the Industrial Era and how we will work in the Fifth Era. They are glimpses into the future of work and the workplace.

Breaking from Assumptions Creates Opportunities

By now, some readers may be saying to themselves that we, the authors of this book, don't understand the importance of physical interactions and in-person relationships and that we are wrong and overstating the prospects of the virtual. Perhaps that is true to some extent. But do be open to challenging your own mindset. What underlying assumptions are you believing? What assumptions are you finding hard to let go? What makes these underlying assumptions "unbreakable" for you? Are the stories you tell yourself really true? Are you sure that Generation C will believe in those assumptions and will share your mindset?

At this juncture let us state an important belief: the people who best capture the opportunity of new and disruptive innovations are those who are best able to disengage from the underlying assumptions of the past, imagine how human activity can be disrupted in the future, and then build the new approaches and companies to bring those to the world.

Disruptive innovators are very good at letting go of the mindsets of the past. They are very good at breaking from assumptions that most of us hold as inviolable.

Take a look at one example of a disrupter who has made a fortune by unlocking a new business model that resulted from his refusal to accept conventional wisdom: Adam Neuman, who founded WeWork in 2010 in New York, recently visited California to discuss further expansion of the company.

To understand WeWork, first let's consider the world of office space. In the world of office space, most people have no choice but to sign multi-year leases on small office spaces, frequently in isolated corridors in large office buildings. In the past, when we accumulated a lot of equipment, filing cabinets, and bookcases, and did most of our work at desks and on the office telephone, a physical office space was typically necessary. This was true both for small firms and new companies starting out.

Adam noticed that the arrival of the digital economy had created a number of new realities that were challenging this old model of office work. For example, today most of us keep most of our information virtually and don't need files, bookcases, and so forth. We transact our business more often than not electronically on mobile devices, not fixed landlines. We don't need large conference rooms, reception areas, and receptionists very often anymore. We just don't need to "own" all of that space all of the time.

Meanwhile, the costs of forming new businesses have fallen, and the next generation of entrepreneurs is more comfortable creating new businesses in serial fashion, starting one after another until something gets traction. They can't be sure how long one entrepreneurial venture will last, so it does not make sense to make long-term commitments for potentially short-lived ventures.

Why should they have to sign a multi-year lease on a space larger than they need? And why should they have to hire dedicated support personnel when the office landlord can provide those people and spread them in support of a host of tenants, thus gaining cost synergies in the process?

Adam saw that the dominant form of office space in the city was ripe for disruption—at least on behalf of a new generation of young entrepreneurial tenants, even if big companies preferred to maintain the multi-year lease model.

So, WeWork was launched as a new flexible office format with pay-as-you-go arrangements and services available on demand. Any individual or company can base itself at a WeWork office location taking as small an amount of space as they need—from a private office, to a dedicated desk, to a "hot desk" shared with others on a first-come, first-served basis each day. This space is taken on a monthly basis, so multi-year contracts are not required. Meanwhile, WeWork provides additional services, such as:

- Super fast Internet
- Access to business printers
- Onsite business support staff
- Free refreshments
- Networking events
- Meetings with experts and investors

Today WeWork has dozens of locations on several continents and a valuation in excess of $16 billion. WeWork is only seven years old as we write. Many believe that flexible workspace is the future and in only a few decades it will replace the old model around the world—at least for those tenants that prefer this new model.

Characteristics of the Fifth Era

These examples, in which long-held human activities built upon underlying assumptions are now being rethought because of the disruptive innovations of our time, are only a few of many. Indeed, every aspect of human existence is being impacted. Some years ago we co-authored a paper on "The Next Wave of Digitization" intended for corporate executives. In it, we summarized the three driving forces that are making this digitization phenomenon possible. The summary of this paper is included as Sidebar 3: Three Driving Forces.

Sidebar 3: Three Driving Forces

The outlines of the fully digitized world have long been sketched. So, why are we reaching this critical inflection point now? The reason is that three driving forces, acting in concert, are powerfully reinforcing one another.

Consumer Pull

Consumers, and particularly Generation C, are already fully adapted to the digital environment. They expect to be connected every moment of their lives, through virtually every device, whether they are consuming news and entertainment, reaching out to their friends through social media, such as Facebook and Twitter, or mixing work with play as they go through the working day. Their insistence on the right to stay connected is transforming their personal lives, and their willingness to share everything is changing long-held attitudes about privacy. Their trust is shifting from well-known brands to referrals from their closest friends. They are advocates of many causes and at the same time deeply embedded in their social environments. In their world, knowledge isn't just power. It's social and commercial currency—and access to it is vital. These changes are forcing companies to rethink how to manage their employees, who are already becoming less emotionally attached to their company's wider purpose and goals and who expect to be able to live their digital lives at work as well as at home. These trends are spreading outward from the developed world, as new middle-class populations in every emerging market are being connected to the global information flow. The typical Generation C consumer now spends a large portion of their day online, always connected, always communicating.

Technology Push

Digital technology continues to make inroads into every aspect of our lives. The infrastructure backbone of the digital world is expanding into every corner of the globe, bringing affordable wired and wireless broadband to billions of consumers in developed and developing markets alike. Three-quarters of the world's population are now connected through mobile phones while digital cloud-based services gather more and more data on consumers in every segment. In parallel with the "Internet of People," low-cost connected sensors and devices are being deployed in every industry. The development of cloud computing and the vast information processing machinery it requires is well under way. As a result, the demand for powerful real-time analytics engines to allow companies to gather and make sense of hitherto "undigested" information flows is rising fast, and companies around the world are responding with new technologies, such as in-memory analytics devices, to meet that need.

Economic Benefits

The third force driving the digitization phenomenon is the realization on the part of executives in every industry that the economic benefits to be captured are real. Though it is too early to quantify those benefits, a wave of capital has poured into the new digitization technologies and companies, and the public markets are beginning to reward early movers with valuations reminiscent of the years leading up to the dot-com bubble. An increasing portion of the $22 billion and the $20 billion that US venture capital firms and US angel investors, respectively, invest each year appears to be going into these digitization technologies. Recent transactions in the secondary financial markets have suggested that Facebook is worth more than $80 billion while LinkedIn recently went public at a valuation of more than $3.3 billion, a high multiple over its 2010 revenues of $243 million. On a national scale, the benefits of digitization created through investments in broadband infrastructure have been amply demonstrated.

Meanwhile, the economic cycle and globalization have exposed the weaknesses of large enterprises that have so far failed to embrace digitization. They have also sharpened the minds of CEOs regarding the need to further cut costs and monetize existing capabilities more effectively. Finally, increased competition from around the world is forcing companies in every industry to contend with increased cost pressures, transforming their traditional value chains, spawning new formats and new business models, blurring industry boundaries, and even creating entirely new industries. In response, companies are turning to digitization to provide a competitive advantage and to generate growth.

At the sovereign level, too, countries and regions are acting to accelerate the digitization phenomenon. China has written cloud, connectivity, and digitization goals into its twelfth five-year plan, which will include stimulus measures estimated at more than $1.7 trillion.

> The European Union has agreed on an energy upgrade plan of more than $200 billion, and the UK's national infrastructure plan earmarks more than $200 billion.
>
> Source: Friedrich, R., Le Merle, M., Peterson, M., & Koster, A. (2011). The next wave of digitization—Setting your direction, building your capabilities. Booz & Company.

The purpose of this chapter is not to detail all of the characteristics of the Fifth Era, but we would like to share our list of the top fifteen characteristics of the Fifth Era that we see as particularly important to watch and track. They are:

Top 15 Characteristics of the Fifth Era

1. The development of an entirely digital world in which information, communication, and collaboration are comprehensive and instantaneous.

2. The invention of new and unimaginable innovations at the intersection of the Digital Revolution and the Biotechnology Revolution and a constant flow of a host of other disruptive innovations feeding off the global availability of knowledge and new collaborative innovation approaches.

3. Addressable target markets rapidly becoming global, allowing disruptive innovations to quickly be adopted by billions of people (assuming our "Wildcard 1: Balkanization of the Global Economic System" does not get played—see below).

4. Consumers gaining enormously as the choices they have will be multiplied by a host of competing solutions and providers, and prices will fall given the economies of scale provided by serving global markets.

5. There will be a reevaluation of what humans value and what makes us happy, with significant implications for markets for consumer goods and services. The next generations may value simplicity/less over clutter/excess and experiences over material goods.

6. A dramatic increase in productivity. But, this time it will not just be increases in labor productivity. Instead, physical asset productivity will also be greatly enhanced, and formerly unproductive assets will be made available for others to use on demand.

7. The Industrial Era large corporate model of organization will be challenged, with the largest companies increasingly extending their enterprises beyond their four walls and looking more like virtual entities.

8. Public markets will need to evolve to address their shortcomings, for example, short termism.

9. Private capital will drive the initial stages of development for most emerging innovations capturing much of the value of new disruptive innovations.

10. Sustainability will become an essential part of doing business with a clear focus on the broader societal impacts of company strategies including the quality of jobs, the full impact of products and services on society and other external considerations.

11. People will have much more freedom to spend their time according to their desires. Multi-tasking, parallel

working, and short-lived organizations and workgroups will be the norm, and the very notion of work will change.

12. Distributed innovation will be everywhere, with no monopoly on innovation by any one company, country, or region. Most innovation will come from small, emerging players, with large corporations being the "go-to-market" partners for innovators.

13. There will be a global war for talent as every digital innovation hub and every region and country try to keep their own technology innovators home and attract those of neighboring regions in order to further strengthen their innovation economies.

14. The power of diversity will be increasingly understood and leveraged.

15. Traditional philanthropy and the for-profit model will come closer together as non-profits look at becoming more sustainable in social entrepreneurship models, and as for-profit corporations aim for double and triple bottom line outcomes.

Because of these changes, every industry, every profit pool, in every country, will be fundamentally challenged as we move into the Fifth Era. We believe that it is possible to already see significant new areas of economic opportunity and wealth creation by divining carefully through these glimpses of the future and making a few bets.

At this point, we expect that many of our readers will be asking, "Why aren't the authors naming the new era? If the second era was called the Agrarian, and the fourth the Industrial, what should be the name of the Fifth Era?" For our part, we think it is too early to say. We know some of the outlines of the future, and we are sure it will be very different from today and driven by the disruptive innovations that we are experiencing today and expect to surface tomorrow—impelled by the twin forces of the Digital and Biotechnology Revolutions. But, there are a lot of plausible futures for how the Fifth Era manifests. We recommend that we simply call it the "Fifth Era" for another twenty or thirty years by which time we expect that the essence of this future era will be coming into clearer focus.

Is the Fifth Era Guaranteed?

At this point in the book, we need to cover our bases. So far, we have driven down one road as quickly as possible, a road we contend is almost certainly going to prove to be the one that society takes over the next few decades. This is the road to the Fifth Era.

But, is it definitely the road to the future? Are there no turnings from it? Is it assured that society will reach this new destination?

We see a few ways in which society could step off the road or at least take a turn that might end up being a dead end or take the long way around to the same destination. We call these "wildcards." Let's share three with you, each of which keeps us up at night because they might just block the road to the Fifth Era.

- Wildcard 1: Balkanization of the Global Economic System
- Wildcard 2: Cybersecurity Crises and Failures
- Wildcard 3: Regulation and Anti-Technology Protectionism

We will briefly review each in turn.

Wildcard 1: Balkanization of the Global Economic System

The Internet is a global phenomenon. It was greatly accelerated by a time of globalization in which most countries in the world agreed to share content, encourage cross-border trade and commerce, and where most people were willing to collaborate with most other people. Holdouts exist of course: the great firewall of China, North Korea's "Kwangmyong" or "Bright" Internet cut off from the rest of the world and hosted in China with perhaps a handful of websites compared to the hundreds of millions on the world's Internet. But, these are the exceptions. Most of the world's 190-plus countries are open to the global Internet and participate more or less in the global economic system.

What would happen to the Fifth Era if this were not true? What if the world went instead in the direction of George Orwell's novel *1984* that features, among other things, three perpetually warring totalitarian super-states that choose not to cooperate with each other?

In George Orwell's novel there are three "balkanized" super-states:

- **Oceania** (Western Hemisphere, the British Isles, Australasia, and Southern Africa)

- **Eurasia** (Continental Europe and Russia, including Siberia)

- **Eastasia** (China, Japan, Korea, and Indochina)

In *1984*, these three states wage a perpetual war in "the disputed area," which is an area encompassing Northern Africa, the Middle East, India, and Indonesia. This is a place of war, slave labor, and constant chaos.

Perhaps, we don't need to go quite that far.

What if the USA/Europe, China and satellites, and Russia and satellites, for example, simply decided to erect firewalls and operate their own Internets behind those firewalls? Three Internets instead of one? With three disconnected bodies of content and separate worlds of commerce and interaction?

And, what if that went a little further? Perhaps, the physical flow of goods and services would be greatly reduced, embargoes, quotas, and tariffs more widespread, and travel, migration (immigration and emigration), and interaction more controlled and limited.

Over time, perhaps, innovation breakthroughs would not be shared, knowledge would not flow, and the world would diverge.

Would we eventually reach the Fifth Era—a globally-connected and collaborating world? Or, would we stop short in a balkanized world?

Would there be less opportunity? Or, would there be three zones of rather smaller opportunity—but more in total?

As we write this in 2017, George Orwell's writings do not seem to be completely lacking in predictive merit.

Wildcard 2: Cybersecurity Crises and Failures

The Internet has transformed every aspect of our content sharing, communications, commerce, and entertainment globally. Today every industry relies upon aspects of the digital economy to conduct their business activities and to connect to other entities: vendors, sales and marketing partners, customers, service vendors, and so on. In addition, new products and services are being built with innovations of the Digital Revolution built into them. Products that rely on the cloud, global positioning systems, cyber authorization, validation and transactional systems and more are now the norm.

Crime has always been a part of human activity, and bad actors and bad practices have always entered the picture whenever large economic gains can be made through illegally attacking legitimate activities. However, just as the Digital Revolution has made legitimate commerce much more easy to effect on a global scale, so the Digital Revolution has also enabled the bad actors. It has also created a host of powerful new weapons for sovereign state actors to use, both in peacetime spying and in states of war, the latter, of course, being the ultimate "wildcard." Mankind could destroy its own ability to operate in a digitally connected way should state actors in a time of war destroy the viability of the digital infrastructure upon which a future era depends.

Meanwhile, private bad actors come in all shapes and sizes. There are those who are principally out for economic gain and may conduct identity theft, scams of all sorts in which they trick others into paying them, fraudulent transactions for commercial activities to their benefit, and so on. There are also bad actors who philosophically disagree with the activities of others—be they at the individual, group, or societal levels. These actors are perhaps more threatening in that they may seek to disrupt new era activities without any need for the underlying digital systems to continue operating after they have completed their bad acts (in marked contrast to the economically motivated bad actors who need the Internet to operate just as much as anyone else). These disruptors are of the greatest threat to the viability of a society that has become dependent upon cyber systems. The unprecedented scale of new technology-enabled criminals has taken authorities by surprise, and in many cases, those that seek to police legitimate activity have been lagging those who seek to criminally take advantage. Viruses, malicious code, identify theft on a massive scale and so on are everyday newspaper headlines today.

In every part of the world, governments are beginning to establish institutions to address this rising tide of cybercrime, and private entities, with their products and services, are also becoming more widespread as money can be made in protecting vulnerable players.

We view this as a wildcard because we are not convinced this battle can be won. Time will tell.

Wildcard 3: Regulation and Anti-Technology Protectionism

The digital economy is driving innovation and growth around the world. As new technologies, business models, and companies are emerging, they are fundamentally altering the business landscape and the ways that traditional industries operate. While this is driving GDP and job growth in most countries, it also provides new challenges to lawmakers. The regulatory landscape has been evolving rapidly as the Internet continues to expand into all areas of business and personal life, and as lawmakers respond to the issues and concerns that are brought to them. While new regulations can potentially boost growth, they also raise the real risk of negatively impacting the investment environment and the success of Internet companies and the growth they represent. Lawmakers are considering new regulations in areas, including 1) copyright and intellectual property, 2) intermediary liability protection and censorship, 3) privacy and security, and 4) mobile infrastructure and services.

In order to ensure that the views of Internet investors are incorporated into the thinking of lawmakers, Fifth Era has conducted surveys in 2011, 2014, and 2016 to determine the impact that potential Internet regulations may have on their investing activities. Our findings have been consistent across all three studies. They are summarized below.

Investors are chilled by regulatory ambiguity and would reduce their capital investment if countries introduce Internet regulations that reduce their investment viability or return.

Exhibit 13

Investors Perception of Legal Environment Impact on Investing

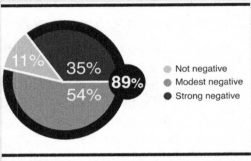

Source: Fifth Era, LLC

Investors are concerned by some potential regulations in areas including:

- **Legal Encroachment:** Globally, investors view the legal environment as having the most negative impact on their investing activities, with 89% of the investors surveyed saying it had a modest or strongly negative impact (see Exhibit 13).

- **Regulatory Ambiguity:** In every country surveyed, a large majority of investors say that they are uncomfortable investing in business models in which the regulatory framework is ambiguous. Of the worldwide investors surveyed, 75% held this view.

- **Security/Surveillance:** 81% of investors would not invest in Internet businesses if government agencies could confiscate properties without court orders.

- **Taxation:** 80% of investors are concerned that countries may apply tax rules that make them subject to double taxation.

- **Freedom of Expression:** 79% of investors are uncomfortable investing in countries where freedom of expression is restricted or highly regulated.

- **Amount of Damages Uncertain:** 78% of investors would not invest in Internet business models in which the amount of damages (in the event of liability) is uncertain or not tiered or staged in relation to the various levels of violation.

- **Law Enforcement Access to Data:** 78% of investors would be deterred from investing in Internet businesses if user data could be disclosed to law enforcement without following international baseline standards.

- **Third-Party Liability:** 71% of investors are uncomfortable investing in Internet businesses where the intermediaries could be held liable for third-party content or actions.

- **Data Storage In-Country:** 67% of investors are uncomfortable investing in Internet businesses that are legally obligated to store user data on servers located in the same country where users are located and/or build their own data centers locally in each country of operations.

- **Site Blocking:** 62% of investors are uncomfortable investing in digital content intermediary businesses (online platforms allowing uploads of user-generated content, including music and video) that would be required by law to run a technological filter on user-uploaded content.

- **Content Removal:** 71% of investors are uncomfortable investing in Internet businesses that would be obligated to remove content upon receiving a request from an organization, private or government entity, without a court order.

- **Traditional Telecom Regulations:** 63% of investors are

uncomfortable investing in Internet/mobile businesses where regulators are applying traditional telecom regulations to new mobile and over-the-top services.

- **Mobile Regulation Reductions:** 77% of investors say that if a country adopts policies aimed at reducing regulations for the mobile apps ecosystem, this would increase their interest in investment in Internet businesses in that country.

More generally, investors say that they would reduce their capital investment in countries that introduce new Internet regulations that may limit the ability of Internet businesses to be attractive investment candidates. As a result, government lawmakers should engage investors in their decision making early to ensure that regulations are not introduced without a full understanding of the potential adverse consequences to investment activity.

Source: Le Merle, M., Davis, A., & Le Merle, F. (2015). The impact of Internet regulation on investment. Fifth Era LLC.

The wildcards are each possible. The Fifth Era is not assured. Humankind holds its own destiny in its hands, and some critical choices are upon us regarding our collective future. In particular, governments can kill our future of innovation and transformation by choosing a world of economic balkanization, government-sponsored cybersecurity attacks, and excessive and suffocating regulation.

However, we believe we will avoid all three wildcards and that the Fifth Era will be our future. It is just a question of how fast it will take to come to pass—and how long the time of transition will last.

In the next part of this book, we turn to the scale of the wealth being created by Fifth Era disrupters, who is playing for that wealth, and who is sitting on the sidelines—so far at least.

Part 2 | Winners and Losers in the Fifth Era

Chapter 4
Who Is Winning?

Innovation distinguishes between a leader and a follower.

—Steve Jobs

We stated in earlier chapters that times of transition between eras create opportunities for enormous economic value creation. This is the result of two factors. On the one hand, disruptive innovations open up new sources of opportunity that did not exist before. On the other, they may shift the playing field such that the capabilities and assets that allowed players to win in the past may no longer be the ones that define success in the future. As a result of these two factors, the subsequent era's wealth creation is potentially open to new players who are bringing new capabilities and resources that are more relevant for the next era. Meanwhile, for those who do not embrace the realities of the new era, times of transition can become periods of massive economic value destruction as we will show in Chapter 5.

We see this quite clearly in the transition phases between prior eras. For example, the Agrarian Era was dominated by people who owned land because land gave the opportunity to deploy the new agricultural innovations of the time. In the shift from the Agrarian Era to the Mercantile Era, wealth was captured by merchants who understood how to use the new technologies of international travel (the age of sail, navigation, and so forth), how to identify goods that could be sold profitably in other geographies, and how to trade for those goods. City-states that were built upon this mercantile mindset formed where these new entrepreneurs clustered together and accumulated their wealth. They were good places to be a merchant. In this transition, we see wealth shift from one group of players with a certain type of capabilities and assets to another who had attributes that better suited the new era.

In this chapter, we will demonstrate that the coming Fifth Era and the time of transition that we are living through is already the greatest economic value creation opportunity that the world has ever seen.

Three Observations about Today's World

As we explore the transition phase we are in and assess the wealth creation that is resulting, we should first make three observations about the state of the world today.

First, the population of the world is larger than it has ever been. When we went through prior transitions between eras, the earth supported a much smaller human population, in the hundreds of millions, or in the case of the Industrial Era, in the small number of billions. But this era that we are now entering sees the global population approaching eight billion. This means we have a much larger number of people passing through the transition (see Exhibit 2 in Chapter 1: The Population Curve).

Second, the economic activity of the world is also higher than it's ever been as witnessed through measures such as GDP per capita. The absolute economic output of the world has never been larger. This means that the economic profit pools being impacted are far larger than in the past.

Exhibit 14
World GDP Per Capita Adjusted for Inflation

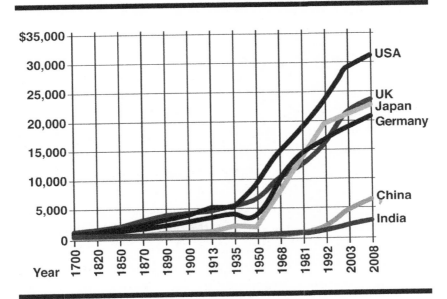

Source: Angus Maddison

Finally, the world is more globally connected than it was in the past. Earlier we described how globalization was not necessarily a one-directional phenomenon, and we walked through the wildcard of how balkanization between continents and nations might unwind globalization. However, the world is far more interconnected today than it has ever been. Addressable markets are larger, and new technologies have the opportunity to capture more profits by serving more people from the moment that they launch.

These simple observations—the population is larger than ever, the combined economic activity is greater than ever, and globalization is at an unprecedented level—are all reasons why we expect that the current time of transition should represent a larger value creation opportunity than any time before.

The world is entering its greatest economic value creation phase of all time.

The World's Most Innovative Companies...

Booz & Company (now PWC Strategy&) has for 12 years conducted a survey of the Global Innovation 1000. These are the one thousand corporations worldwide that spend the most on research and development. In 2016 these companies spent an incredible $680 billion on these activities. Every year the authors ask the chief innovation or research and development officers at each company to rank those other companies that they believe are most innovative. Exhibit 15 shows the results in 2016. Most of the top ten are disruptive innovation companies that have either been born into the transition to the Fifth Era or have fully embraced it within their cultures and approaches. The top five are listed below.

- Apple takes first position in 2016, spending $8.1 billion on research and development across its family of computing hardware, software, and services. Founded in Cupertino by Steve Jobs, Steve Wozniak, and Ronald Wayne in 1976, Apple has been successful at bringing to market a series of disruptive innovations beginning with its first personal computers, through its iPod music player, iTunes platform, and into its iPhone and iPad family of products where today it ships more mobile phone devices than any other company except Samsung.

- Second on the list is Alphabet/Google. Google was founded by Larry Page and Sergey Brin in 1996 on the Stanford University campus as the two developed a new approach to Internet search. The company went public in 2004, and then in 2016 a new public holding company, Alphabet, was created. The company is an innovator across many digital domains including cloud computing, big data analytics and algorithms, artificial intelligence, computer recognition, robotics, drones, AR/VR, and many others.

- 3M is the oldest company in the top 5, having been formed in 1905 in Minnesota. Originally the Minnesota Mining and Manufacturing Company, 3M is famous for always emphasizing innovation across every category it competes in, including adhesives, abrasives, laminates, passive fire protection, dental and orthodontic products, electronic materials, medical products, and car-care products. 3M has been profiled as a leader in innovation and new product development for at least 50 years. Inge Thulin is the company's current CEO.

- Tesla Motors is the newest company on the list, founded in 2003 and focused on electric vehicles, energy storage, and solar energy. Tesla's first commercial product, the Tesla Roadster, was only launched in 2008 with an AC motor derived from Nikola Tesla's 1882 design—hence, the company's name. Today Tesla's CEO is Elon Musk, and the company is viewed as a disruptive innovator across the industries in which it competes.

- Amazon was founded in 1994 by Jeff Bezos who continues to be CEO today. Seattle-based Amazon.com is the largest Internet retailer in the world by sales and is a leader in cloud computing where it offers its services to enable other companies to move their information technology to the cloud. Amazon is viewed as a very active innovator in online commerce, digital content, cloud computing, distributed computing, logistics, drone delivery, and other domains.

Rounding out the top ten list are Samsung of Korea and four other US companies: Facebook, Microsoft, General Electric, and IBM.

Exhibit 15

2016: Top 10 Most Innovative Companies

2016 Rank	Company	Geography	Industry	R&D Spend ($Bn)*
1	Apple	United States	Computing & Electronics	8.1
1	Alphabet	United States	Software & Internet	12.3
3	3M	United States	Industrials	1.8
4	Tesla Motors	United States	Automotive	0.7
5	Amazon	United States	Software & Internet	12.5
6	Samsung	South Korea	Computing & Electronics	12.7
7	Facebook	United States	Software & Internet	4.8
8	Microsoft	United States	Software & Internet	12.0
9	General Electric	United States	Industrials	4.2
10	IBM	United States	Computing & Electronics	5.2

*R&D spend data is based on the most recent full-year figures reported prior to July 1st
Source: PWC Strategy&

Of these most innovative companies, six are headquartered in the Western United States with four in California in the San Francisco Bay Area (Apple, Alphabet/Google, Facebook, and Tesla Motors) and two in Washington State (Amazon and Microsoft).

Throughout this book we will refer to these six as our **"Most Innovative Companies,"** and the findings in this book are heavily derived from the activities and behaviors of these companies and the people who lead and work at them. We have been fortunate to learn about these six as we have interacted with them as advisors, consultants, investors, partners, and observers. We have also selectively added other examples and case studies from additional innovative companies and players throughout the book—but the heart of the new corporate innovation approach we describe is derived from these six.

...Are Also the Most Valuable

The majority of the large companies in the world today are public companies, and as a result, their market capitalizations can be measured in the public markets. For the last hundred years or so, the most valuable companies on those lists were industrial companies and resource-heavy companies. They were the big industrial companies such as General Electric and IBM in America. They were the large, resource-heavy companies, such as the oil majors including ExxonMobil and Shell, and more recently the Chinese oil company Sinopec. And they were also the large, multinational financial institutions that supported the Industrial Era and the trading and financial activity that the large companies were engaged in. And so we saw on the lists the names of banks, like Bank of America, Royal Bank of Scotland, and Wells Fargo, and more recently Chinese banks, including Industrial and Commercial Bank of China, China Construction Bank Corporation, and Agricultural Bank of China.

Today, if we review a list of the world's most valuable companies by market capitalization, it looks markedly different. Take a look:

Exhibit 16

Largest Companies by Market Capitalization

Symbol	Company	Cap Rank on 2/28/17	Market Cap on 2/28/17
AAPL	Apple	1	718.7
GOOGL	Alphabet	2	584.2
MSFT	Microsoft	3	494.4
BRK-A	Berkshire Hathaway	4	423.4
AMZN	Amazon.com	5	403.2
FB	Facebook	6	391.7
XOM	Exxon Mobil	7	337.2
JNJ	Johnson & Johnson	8	332.5
JPM	JPMorgan Chase	9	323.6
WFC	Wells Fargo	10	290.3

Source: Dogsofthedow.com

No less than five of the six most valuable companies in the world are also on our list of most innovative companies. They are Alphabet/Google, Amazon, Apple, Facebook, and Microsoft. Only Tesla, the newest company on the most innovative ranking, fails to also make it to the list of most valuable companies. Meanwhile, Warren Buffet's Berkshire Hathaway rounds out the top six.

We don't believe it is a coincidence that the most valuable companies in the world are also the most innovative.

These companies, Apple, Alphabet/Google, Microsoft,

Amazon, and Facebook, in particular, have risen to become the most valuable companies in the world, and that's not simply because they have large revenues and profit pools today. Of course they do. Apple has revenue of $214.2B, driving an incredible annual net income of $45.7B. Alphabet, driven by the Google search machine, has revenue of $89.7B and net income of $19.5B. The second reason why these companies are so valuable is because the world's investors view them as the companies best positioned to capitalize on the coming Fifth Era, which is evidenced in their high P/E ratios and the expectations of a great deal of future growth that these companies will capture.

No less than five of the six most valuable companies in the world today are technology companies, and additional technology companies fill out the list further down the rankings beyond the top ten. Not only are the most valuable companies in the world technology companies, but most of them are new Fifth Era technology companies with more of a leg in the new Fifth Era world—the connected, interactive world as described in Part 1—and a relatively smaller foot in the Industrial Era computing phase, although Apple and Microsoft began in the computer phase of the Industrial Era.

Indeed, when we look at Apple or Microsoft, they increasingly put more emphasis on the Internet and the new, emerging computer and content technologies, and they have begun to scale back and even exit the legacy computing environments of the past where they were first founded. Amazon, Alphabet/Google, and Facebook conversely are all children of this transition phase, and their businesses are almost entirely built upon new, emerging, and disruptive technologies.

These companies are, for the most part, also at the frontier of many of the disruptive innovations described in Part 1. As an example, we see Apple exploring new data analytics and artificial intelligence algorithms, continuing to expand its content portals and payments approaches, and exploring self-driving vehicles and other coming disruptive innovations.

Alphabet has gone so far as to split its company essentially into two parts, with Google continuing to operate the very large, but relatively new businesses that it built as part of the Digital Revolution. Those new businesses include areas such as search, video sharing through YouTube, email through Gmail, and so on. Meanwhile, the other half of Alphabet is entirely focused on creating businesses in the areas of new disruptive innovations that we described above. Alphabet is making substantial investments and inroads into areas as diverse as self-driving vehicles, robotics, artificial intelligence, genomics, and more, and calls them "moonshots."

These observations—that the world's most valuable companies are today Fifth Era technology companies, that the public market investors expect these companies to show the greatest growth of the large companies in the world, and that these companies in themselves are betting so heavily on new areas of disruptive innovation—should not be taken lightly. But this is the first of many observations we'll make about why this transition phase is already proving to be the world's greatest wealth-creation opportunity.

In this chapter, we reviewed evidence that the most innovative companies in the world are innovation-focused companies and that the public markets view these as the most valuable companies expecting them to grow at the fastest rate among large corporations.

Now let's look at the economic-value losers during this same timeframe, since times of transition have proven to destroy economic value for those companies that do not adjust to the new realities.

Chapter 5
Why Companies Fail

*It's fine to celebrate success but it is more
important to heed the lessons of failure.*

—*Bill Gates*

If the current rankings of the most valuable companies give an
indication of who is creating economic value, then which companies are losing it and why? That is what we will address in this
chapter.

Heed the Lessons of Failure

In 2012, we co-authored a report that looked at the other half
of the coin (Sidebar 3: The Lessons of Lost Value). Along with
our co-authors, Chris Dann and Chris Pencavel, we collectively
aimed to determine whether the very significant investments our
large corporate clients were making into risk management and
compliance organizations, tools and processes were aligned with
the root causes of economic value losses.

Following some very large and visible corporate failures of
the first part of this century, including Enron, Tyco, and World-
Com, there had been a focused effort in the US to make large
companies more compliant with laws and regulations of all types.
This included the implementation of the Sarbanes-Oxley (SOX)
Act, which created the Public Company Accounting Oversight
Board to oversee public accounting firms in order to ensure,

among other things, that their clients are properly meeting audit standards. The SOX Act allows the power for the oversight board to bring enforcement actions in conjunction with the Securities and Exchange Commission. Secondly, the Act introduced a number of very specific requirements for corporate governance such as the enforcement of fully independent audit committees.

After the 2008 financial crisis, a second wave of new regulatory action was implemented with a particular focus on the financial sector including, for example, the Dodd-Frank Wall Street Reform and Consumer Protection Act. Similar to Sarbanes-Oxley before it, this act was intended to ensure that large companies do a better job of consistently living up to the laws and policies created to ensure proper behavior and reduce the risk of transgressions.

Companies responded to this increased scrutiny by investing heavily in teams of people to drive these and other new policies, processes, and practices across their activities. They also implemented their own policies and practices to ensure that the third parties that they do business with are also compliant: upstream sources of inputs, parallel and downstream go-to-market partners, and all sorts of service providers.

Our intuition was that this effort was not fully aligned with the root causes of corporate failure and that while avoiding breaking rules is itself an appropriate goal, the larger mission should be to avoid corporate failure.

This then raises important research questions. Are corporate failures a result of compliance failures? If not, what does cause them? And what, if any, additional enhancements can be made to corporate risk management to make it meet the larger goal of helping companies avoid failure, for example, by adding methodologies that monitor and mitigate other forms of risk, especially strategic and innovation risk?

Biggest Losers Don't Strategically Innovate

To get at this question we analyzed the biggest losers of economic value over a ten-year period from 2002 to 2012 (Sidebar 3: The Lessons of Lost Value).

The study showed that for the 103 biggest losers of economic value out of all public companies analyzed over the timeframe, over 80% of the time the reason for the significant value destruction was a strategic and/or innovation blunder, for example, being caught by surprise by a disruptive innovation launched by a competitor or new player, or by a strategic inability for a company to keep up with innovations in its industry. This was in marked contrast to the much smaller count of biggest losers who had seen their economic value decline because of risks encountered in the other three categories we analyzed. The four categories of risk include the following:

- Strategic business risks, such as a failure to stay competitive with new innovative products or competitor strategies
- Operations risks, such as supply chain disruptions, customer service breakdowns, etc.
- Fraud, accounting, or ethics violations and other such bad practices
- External shocks that were natural, political, or regulatory in nature

The study emphasized to an even greater degree than we had expected that large corporate economic value declines come from an inability of the company to create innovative strategies that ensure winning in highly competitive and dynamic industry settings.

In short, while the winners in economic value creation are the most innovative companies of the Fifth Era, the losers appear to be those that can't keep up with the new strategies of their industries and competitors: they are laggards in innovation in one way or another.

The Fifth Era and the time of transition we are going through is by definition a time of enormous change and dynamism in most industries. The stakes on corporate innovation have never been higher.

Chapter 8 outlines some of the methodologies proposed to help large companies become better at surfacing strategic risks. However, the larger point is the focus of this book: to avoid economic value losses and stay relevant and vibrant, large companies need to become more intensely focused on innovation across everything they do and pursue a new approach to corporate innovation, taking on board best practices from the world's innovation leaders.

Sidebar 4: The Lessons of Lost Value

While many benchmarks of corporate practice start by looking at successful companies, a recent Booz & Company survey took the opposite tack. We decided to study the biggest losers: companies that, in one way or another, had seen their fortunes go south over a 10-year period. We had gone through this exercise once before. In 2004, when the Enron, Tyco, and WorldCom scandals were fresh, we surveyed thousands of public companies and determined that, contrary to prevailing wisdom, it was not compliance issues that were most responsible for destroying shareholder value. That distinction went to the mismanagement of strategic risks—those risks embedded in the top-level decisions made by the executive team, such as what products and services to offer, whether to outsource manufacturing, or what acquisitions to make.

Our 2012 survey revealed the same culprit and suggested that it still leads to significant value destruction. Making matters worse, the sources of strategic risk have increased. Accelerating technology development is forcing the rapid adoption of new products, services, and business models; digital information is making organizations more vulnerable to theft and loss; supply chain disruptions quickly ripple around the globe, affecting both companies and customers; consumer connectivity via social networks can broadcast missteps instantaneously to millions of people worldwide; and natural, political, or regulatory shocks can reverberate widely. Companies must learn how to effectively anticipate and hedge against these and other risks in order to survive.

Studying the Biggest Losers

To more fully support this conclusion—that the lack of attention to risk destroys shareholder value—we must look at our study in more detail. We analyzed US public companies with at least US$1 billion in enterprise value on January 1, 2002 (1,053 companies met these criteria). We calculated each company's change in enterprise value over the next 10 years and then indexed each company's annualized return to that of its industry benchmark to control for industry-specific effects. This allowed us to zero in on the biggest losers—the companies that experienced the most dramatic losses of enterprise value. Only 103 companies had annualized returns relative to their respective industry benchmarks that were worse than negative 10 percent. This group corresponded to the bottom 10 percent of performers in our overall sample.

We checked to see if the companies on our list of the biggest losers were simply the weakest companies in one or two industries in terminal decline. But this was not the case. There was broad industry representation among the bottom performers.

Next, to get at the root cause of this lost value, we conducted an event analysis by going back to news reports, press articles, and brokerage reports for each of the 103 companies before and after their loss of value. We then assigned each company's economic decline to one of four categories.

The first category included major strategic blunders (such as new product or new market failures) or instances when a company was caught flat-footed by a major industry shift (such as digitization of content). We included failed mergers and acquisitions in this category, as well as dramatic shifts in major enterprise value drivers (for example, a major input cost) because these occurrences should have been foreseen. This category includes, for example, Time Warner and its widely criticized merger with AOL in 2000.

In the second category, we grouped together major operational problems, such as supply chain disruptions, customer service breakdowns, and operational accidents, that had caused substantial shareholder value destruction. A high profile example is the April 2010 Deepwater Horizon offshore oil rig explosion and leaks in the Gulf Coast, an event that wiped out more than $50 billion in BP's shareholder value in the days and weeks following the accident.

The third category included fraud, accounting problems, ethics violations, and other failures to comply with laws, standards, or ethics. During the 10-year timeframe we analyzed, a few prominent examples were Tyco's accounting and discrimination lawsuits in 2002 and Tenet Healthcare's 2006 legal battles over improper medical and business practices.

In the fourth category, we identified declines resulting from external shocks that were natural, political, or regulatory. We narrowed these situations down to circumstances in which the external event could not be controlled or easily anticipated by the company. For example, USEC, a supplier of enriched uranium for nuclear power plants, saw a sudden and sharp decline in enterprise value after the 2011 Japanese tsunami and ensuing nuclear disaster.

The results are unambiguous: among the 103 companies studied, strategic blunders were the primary culprit a remarkable 81% of the time. When we segmented the data by industry and geography, we found some variations; for example, strategic failures are particularly acute in the financial-services industry, and Europe has more operational problems than the US or Asia. Nevertheless, strategic failure remained the major cause in these cases as well.

About half the time, the loss of value occurred gradually: over many months, or even years if the company took too long to grasp a changed strategic environment or lacked the agility to react. The other half of the time, the lost value occurred in a matter of months, weeks, or even days. Sometimes these sharp shocks were caused by strategic failure (for example, being caught by surprise when a competitor introduced a superior product), and sometimes they resulted from an operational issue, compliance problem, or external event that overwhelmed the company.

Source: Dann, C., Le Merle, M., & Pencavel, C. (2012). The lesson of lost value.

In this chapter we showed that the companies that have lost most economic value during the last decades have been those that did not innovate their strategies and were either taken by surprise by new competitor products, services, and approaches, or simply fell behind the requirements to compete.

In the next chapter we will examine the most innovative companies to see what lessons we can learn. What are they doing to be innovative across their businesses? Are there common themes? If so, how can other companies adopt some of those best practices in their own businesses?

Chapter 6
Lessons from the Winners

The nature of an innovation is that it will arise at a fringe where it can afford to become prevalent enough to establish its usefulness without being overwhelmed by the inertia of the orthodox system.

—Kevin Kelly

Many of the lessons that underpin this book's approach to corporate innovation have been learned from the most innovative companies in the world, including Alphabet/Google, Amazon, Apple, Facebook, and Microsoft, and from our interactions with them as advisors, consultants, investors, partners, and observers. On close examination, we have concluded these companies do indeed have a very different approach to corporate innovation. We have also included insights from other successful, high growth companies in the disruptive innovation economy of California and the Western United States who pursue similar approaches to fuel their success. These include companies such as AirBnB, Eventbrite, Fiserv, PayPal, StubHub, Tencent, Tesla, and Xoom that in some cases didn't exist 5 and 10 years ago, but have built successful franchises and multibillion-dollar valuations by leveraging new technologies to create innovative products and services that have been rapidly adopted by customers.

The usefulness of the new approach is apparent when viewed through the lenses of innovation and economic value as shown in Chapters 4 and 5. However, what is striking is not that the elements of the approach are new or unheard of – indeed many of them seem like common sense and are familiar to many other companies including those within the Global Innovation 1000. Many companies are executing elements of the new approach and have been doing so for many years.

Rather what is striking is the degree to which the most innovative companies have implemented every one of the elements of the approach and have a deep passion for innovation that inspires the entire workforce as well as partners, suppliers and others the company comes into contact with. What is also striking is the degree to which the focus is on external innovation beyond the confines of the corporate structure and the degree to which the companies are externally focused.

The new approach is as much about leadership and culture as it is about strategy and implementation. This alignment of leadership, strategy, and culture elevated to the level of a shared corporate value around innovation and external focus drives each company in its entirety, making innovation the central theme.

The rest of this book describes the lessons of these most innovative companies and the new approach to corporate innovation they have adopted.

Corporate Innovation Survey

In order to best prepare for the next few chapters, we encourage you to take a moment and complete the following short survey. By doing so, you will have a summary diagnostic of your own company, which will then allow you to better compare your approach to corporate innovation with the one that we will be describing.

Corporate Innovation Survey

Please respond to the following questions, many of which require *yes* or *no* responses. Based on your responses, you will see how you compare to the new corporate innovation approach, as well as have a baseline with which to compare yourself during the following chapters.

Drive Innovation Top-Down

1. Is your CEO also your chief innovation officer? Yes/No
2. Is innovation prominently featured on the CEO and board agendas? Yes/No
3. Do you see your executive leadership team living innovation in their actions and behaviors? Yes/No
4. Are your leaders passionate about encouraging the organization to be innovative? Yes/No

Embed Innovation into Strategies and Plans

5. Do you have a clearly defined innovation strategy? Yes/No
6. Is your business strategy fully aligned with your innovation strategy? Yes/No
7. Do your business unit leaders believe they own the innovation strategy too? Yes/No

Build an Innovation Culture

8. Does your corporate culture support your innovation strategy? Yes/No
9. Are you customer-driven in your innovation approach? Yes/No
10. Should all employees be able to innovate products and services offered? Yes/No

11. What percent of your employees do have a mandate to innovate products and services? X = ___%
12. What does innovation as a shared value mean to the rest of your people?

Exploit External Innovation

13. Do you have a well-developed external innovation strategy? Yes/No
14. Over the next decade where will the most important innovations in your industry come from?
    a. Your company
    b. Your industry
    c. Outside your industry
15. What percentage of your innovation spend is internal vs. external—people and capital? ___%
16. What percentage of your innovation spend focuses beyond your industry? _____%

Self-Scoring

Please add up the number of *yes* answers you gave in questions 1, 2, 3, 4, 5, 6, 7, 8, 9, and 13.

10 out of 10—Your corporate innovation approach is like that of the most innovative companies.

7 to 9 inclusive—You can implement additional best practices of the most innovative companies.

Less than 6—You have an urgent need to transform your corporate innovation approach.

Please keep your answers at hand as you continue to read the book.

Disruptive and Incremental Innovation

Early in writing this book we thought we needed to decide whether we would focus on disruptive or incremental innovation. That is, we thought we needed to determine whether to focus on the innovations that change entire markets and industries, and sometimes create entirely new ones; or conversely, whether to focus on innovation as it takes place every day in companies as they work to make each current product, service, and activity a little bit better within the competitive environment of today.

In order to decide where to focus, we asked leaders in the most innovative companies to explain how they differentiate the two: disruptive versus incremental innovation. We were surprised by their answers because they did not seem to recognize the distinction as being of primary value.

One Microsoft executive put it this way: "We view innovation as being the process and customer benefit as being the objective function. Whether a given innovation ends up being disruptive or incremental is a result of the impact that the innovation has on meeting customer needs. We can't begin by trying to predict whether an innovation will be disruptive or not. The result of innovation is an output variable—sometimes disruptive and sometimes incremental—but not something we know in advance."

An Apple executive put it this way: "We could see that the MP3 technology was superior for small external storage devices and given our focus on improving the customer experience across every personal computing device, we knew we needed to be there. But the brilliance of the team was to see how to disrupt the entire music industry by combining a new mobile storage device (the iPod) with an easy way to download your music to it (iTunes). It turned out to be a disruptive innovation, but we did not begin expecting that to be the case."

This seems to be the common refrain of the most innovative

companies. They track new and emerging domains of technology that appear to bring the prospect of positively impacting the customer, and they work with those technologies to see what can be done. They also observe closely their competitors and what use they put these same technologies to. They make sure every improvement is in their products and services too—all of the time. They are paranoid about missing a big disruptive technology.

Sometimes they are surprised in both directions. An innovation they thought would change the world goes belly up, like the Apple Newton, which was a too-early version of a smartphone, or Google Orkut, which lost out to Facebook. Conversely, they launch what they thought would be a modest success and are surprised by the world adopting it, like the famous example of IBM launching its personal computers expecting a modest market potential, only to find one on every desk a decade or two later. This was an unexpected success that drove Microsoft to its position as the world's leading operating system as part of the Wintel (Windows, Intel) platform.

The most innovative companies appear to make innovation the theme and don't worry quite so much about whether it is incremental or disruptive. At the same time, and as we will show in Chapter 10, they believe that disruptive innovations most usually come from outside their own company, so they work very hard to ensure they are knowledgeable about and active in all of the places where disruptive innovation might surface. They use all of the external innovation tools we will outline in Chapter 11.

For the most part, they don't make this a separate approach: they don't have an incremental and a disruptive innovation program. Instead, they define areas of opportunity and work to understand and exploit all innovations that can help, always driven by the objective function of making things better for customers, whether it is incremental or transformational.

At Amazon, this is very clear. While the company and its innovators are supported in taking very long-term views, and Jeff Bezos constantly encourages risk-taking and failure, there is also a constant focus on making incremental improvements, however small, if they can be shown to materially improve customer experience and internal operations. As Bezos once remarked, "A big piece of the story we tell ourselves about who we are, is that we are willing to invest. We are willing to think long term. We start with the customer and work backward. And very importantly we are willing to be misunderstood for long periods of time." He goes on to note, "You can [also] do incremental invention, which is critically important for any company."

We take this view in the rest of this book. There are certainly exceptions where an innovation domain is explored because it is likely to be disruptive if it eventually succeeds in delivering products and services that can be brought to market. Sometimes this is broken off as a separate initiative. But the central theme of the new corporate innovation approach is not to decide in advance whether to drive incremental improvements or to seek out disruptive ones.

Rather, it is to do both within one core approach that we now describe.

Overview of the Approach

The lessons of the most innovative companies have been summarized in a new corporate innovation approach that comprises four main elements. The most innovative companies consistently do all four of them, and they do so with a passion and zeal that is remarkable to observe. It is not just a question of implementing all four elements. It is a matter of the intensity and central focus with which they are pursued.

This corporate innovation approach is illustrated in Exhibit 17.

Exhibit 17

**Four Main Elements of the Fifth Era Corporate
Innovation Approach**

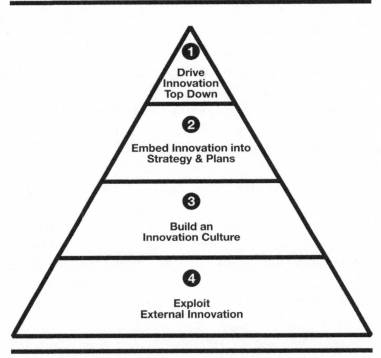

Source: Fifth Era, LLC

1. **Drive Innovation Top-Down.** At the most innovative
   companies, innovation is a priority focus at the very top
   of the company – driven by the CEO and executive team
   and with active interest and input from the board of directors. Innovation is driven top-down—as leaders live it in
   their own actions and behaviors and by requiring others
   to understand the environment and think about and plan
   for the future.

2. **Embed Innovation into Strategies and Plans.** The second element is the extent to which the innovation strategy is developed and embedded into plans and actions across all corporate businesses and functions.

3. **Build an Innovation Culture.** The third element is the creation of a culture that supports innovation and in which every employee, from the top leadership to the functions and frontline staff, is passionate, spirited, and driven towards finding superior and innovative ways to serve customers better than their competitors do. This ensures a high degree of alignment between the culture of the company and the innovation strategy.

4. **Exploit External Innovation.** The final element that makes up the new approach to innovation is a refocusing of innovation activities to ensure that they are driven externally versus internally. The most innovative companies are tapping into the world's innovators and their innovations rather than relying on breakthroughs created within the four walls of their own corporations.

The good news is that this new approach is one which every company can apply to benefit from the innovations of the Fifth Era.

The next chapters provide the details of the new approach, specifically:

- Chapter 7 examines how corporate leaders **drive innovation top-down**.
- Chapter 8 briefly describes how to **embed innovation into strategies and plans**.
- Chapter 9 explains how to **build an innovation culture**.

- Chapter 10 looks at how best to **exploit external innovation**.
- Chapter 11 profiles 17 tools in the **external innovation toolkit**.

It will become apparent that this approach to corporate innovation engages everyone in the company. In innovation-driven companies, everyone is engaged, passionate, spirited, and driven by a clear innovation rallying cry.

Part 3: | The New Corporate Innovation Approach

Chapter 7
Drive Innovation Top-Down

If the highest aim of a captain were to preserve his ship, he would keep it in port forever.

—Thomas Aquinas

Over the last decade, the most innovative companies have elevated innovation into the corporate suite and ensure that it is constantly in front of the board of directors and the chief executive officer's (CEO's) executive management team. They then drive innovation top-down, both as leaders living it in their own actions and behaviors, and by asking others to think about and plan for the future. The most innovative companies bake top-down innovation leadership into their new corporation innovation approach.

The leaders of these companies are always asking their people to start a new voyage and not to worry about rocking the boat. As the Thomas Aquinas quote suggests, they don't focus on preserving their ship—they want it to constantly become a better one.

When we talk about leadership, we include all of those people responsible for establishing the vision, mission, and strategies, including driving the everyday operations and ensuring that all supporting requirements of the company are in place and function well. In most large companies this will include both the executive team—the CEO and their direct reports—and the board of directors. The board is important because CEO tenures can be quite short and it is the board that is responsible for the longer-term health and success of the company across the tenure of successive CEOs and leadership team members

Leadership Team Is the Innovation Champion

In the most innovative companies, the entire leadership team, including the board, has a clear view of the innovations that the company is driving or which could most support or threaten the company's future success.

At Facebook, for example, Mark Zuckerberg and his team have defined an innovation strategy that focuses on three future innovation domains which they believe are fundamental to achieving their mission to "Give people the power to share and make the world more open and connected." These three innovation domains are:

- **Connectivity**—including terrestrial solutions, Telco infrastructure, free basics, satellites, drones, and lasers
- **Artificial Intelligence**—including vision, language, reasoning, and planning
- **VR/AR**—including social VR, mobile VR, Oculus Rift, touch, and AR technologies

This list of innovation domains is well understood by the entire Facebook management team and board who are actively exploring and communicating about these exciting topics. Mark Zuckerberg himself is a thought leader in these coming areas of innovation; when he speaks both within the company and to external audiences about them, he also discusses their collective impact on the coming digital future and the resulting connected world. He has also been a visionary around the risks of not enabling all of humanity to access such benefits and most recently has needed to address the risks of communities that become disconnected or unsafe to everyone.

At Amazon, Jeff Bezos is just as active, and his external speeches are often focused on the domains of innovation that comprise Amazon's future strategy. He is an active speaker on

behalf of the other companies that he has founded or supported, including Blue Origin, a rocket platform company. In this he
shares a passion with Elon Musk of Tesla, who is perhaps the most
active CEO speaker in the coming world of clean and self-driving
vehicles, alternative renewable power, and space travel—though
again the Alphabet/Google founders, Larry Page and Sergey Brin,
are not far behind since these are also three "moonshots" in the
Alphabet X innovation strategy.

Apple's CEO Tim Cook recently revised Apple's vision and
mission statement to further emphasize the central position of
customer-focused innovation. He writes, "We believe that we
are on the face of the earth to make great products and that's not
changing. We are constantly focusing on innovating. We believe
in the simple, not the complex. We believe that we need to own
and control the primary technologies behind the products that
we make and participate only in markets where we can make a
significant contribution. We believe in saying no to thousands of
projects so that we can really focus on the few that are truly important and meaningful to us. We believe in deep collaboration
and cross-pollination of our groups, which allow us to innovate in
a way that others cannot. And frankly, we don't settle for anything
less than excellence in every group in the company, and we have
the self-honesty to admit when we're wrong and the courage to
change. And I think regardless of who is in what job those values
are so embedded in this company that Apple will do extremely
well."

Everywhere we look, we see the leaders of the most innovative companies speaking about the innovations of the future and
their respective company's strategy in each area. And by doing so,
they align and motivate the rest of their leadership teams to do
the same.

This is in marked contrast to many companies where few
of the most senior people in the company can engage in that

dialogue. To test this, just ask them a simple question, "What is your corporate innovation strategy?" and see how different members of the leadership team (including the board) respond. If they don't sound somewhat similar, there is no alignment among the leadership team, so there can be no shared innovation strategy for the company.

In 2012 we co-authored a report with the San Francisco Bay Area Council, which is the leading economic development organization in Northern California, entitled "The Culture of Innovation: What Makes San Francisco Bay Area Companies Different?" (Jaruzelski, Le Merle, & Randolph, 2012). In that report, we analyzed the most innovative companies in Silicon Valley and compared them with the biggest R&D spenders worldwide that Booz & Company surveys annually for their Global Innovation 1000 report. Exhibit 18 shows that in the highest-spending R&D companies in the world (the Global Innovation 1000), the innovation strategy agenda is most frequently (59.2% of the time) developed and communicated by the senior levels of the organization. In interviews since 2012 with companies that are not in the Global Innovation 1000 we found much lower levels of response on this issue, with a much higher percentage responding that either they do not have an innovation strategy at all or that it is being developed and communicated out of the technical organization rather than the leadership team.

Exhibit 18
How an Organization's Innovation Strategy
Is Developed and Communicated

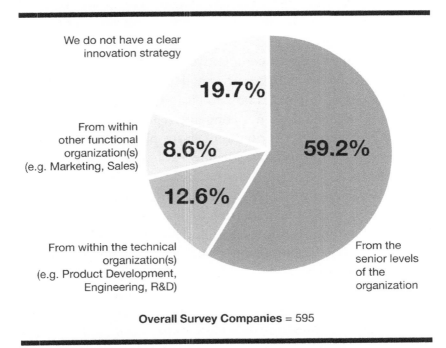

We do not have a clear
innovation strategy

19.7%

From within
other functional
organization(s)
(e.g. Marketing, Sales)

8.6%

59.2%

12.6%

From within the technical
organization(s)
(e.g. Product Development,
Engineering, R&D)

From the
senior levels
of the
organization

Overall Survey Companies = 595

Sources: Bay Area Council Economic Institute, Booz & Company analysis

This top-level engagement and understanding, which results in top-down innovation leadership, is driven in a number of ways by the most innovative companies.

Disruptive Innovation on Every Agenda

The new corporate innovation approach begins with innovation having a regular place on the CEO and board agendas. This is not a novel thought. In prior periods we have seen cost, quality, diversity, compliance, and other topics placed on every agenda where the board and/or executive management team are spending time together specifically to create focus. For example, Proctor and Gamble has encouraged a shared value of "winning" and "competitiveness" in which every P&G employee knows they need to find superior and valuable claims for their products to ensure that they are fully competitive and the leaders in their categories. Meanwhile, Chevron has had a "safety moment" before every meeting for decades now to ensure that every employee is thoughtful about safety in a company that fears major drilling, pipeline, refinery, or distribution catastrophes in their business. While not perfect, this has made safety a shared value of the company.

By making innovation a central agenda topic, the entire team must be prepared in each meeting to discuss where they are with regard to their innovation strategy and plans. This, in turn, begins a trickle-down effect because to be prepared, questions have to be asked, information gathered and analyzed, implications extracted, and gaps, shortfalls, and inadequacies prioritized. The simple act of having innovation be central on the agenda whenever the leadership team is coming together gets the whole ball rolling.

An example of this in action was at Xoom, the innovative money transfer company founded by Kevin Hartz and Alan Braverman, backed by Sequoia and NEA, and sold to PayPal in 2015. Delighting customers – the people who had left their country of origin and were sending money home to family on a regular basis –was a clear passion and focus of CEO John Kunz and the entire leadership team. The entire board of directors frequently engaged in examining how Xoom's products and services fell short and could be continually improved to better delight customers. The board would spend time on root cause analyses of customer churn rates, details of redesigned landing pages to increase click-through rates, the details of call-center dropped call rates and initiatives to improve them, and many other improvement opportunities. This was strategy in action, the daily passion for making the offering better and better every day.

Most companies don't have this as the norm. Indeed many only have innovation on the agenda on an annual basis at major offsites and retreats, and it is more of a sideline and not integrated into everything the company does.

Leaders Make Innovation Their Homework

In the most innovative companies, each member of the leadership team makes innovation their own personal homework. They do this because they are passionate about innovation and because it is their business. They want to know what breakthroughs are coming, what competitors are up to, what other industries are doing, and how all of those innovations might be beneficial to the company and its customers, products, services, and operations. The inclusion of innovation as a priority on the agenda gets everyone's attention.

We met with three of the senior leaders of Axel Springer, Germany's leading publisher and owner of *Bild* and *Die Welt*, when they came to live for six months in Silicon Valley. They had come to immerse the company in the emerging innovations of the digital age and to personally become much more knowledgeable about innovations that might be valuable to Axel Springer as it continues its transformation into a digital media empire.

This is not a one-time exercise, of course. Constantly iterating your viewpoint is critical where innovation is concerned because it is always a moving target. It is a major commitment for any leader to keep abreast of innovations at the same time as doing everything else they are expected to do. But we don't see an alternative. Leaders can't outsource innovation to others, and can't fake it. As J.R.R. Tolkien put it, "Shortcuts make long delays."

The most innovative companies have leaders who are regularly engaged in places where disruptive innovation is happening, being discussed, and being imagined. Some companies bring their entire teams on learning journeys to meet with innovative companies, people, and places. In the case of Axel Springer they brought a larger group to Silicon Valley once the relevant areas of innovation had been scouted by their three resident leaders; today they continue to feed their innovation strategy in Europe with the findings they gain abroad.

Royal Bank of Scotland's leadership is also very active in learning as part of its innovation and transformation strategy. For the last several years RBS has stationed a small team in Silicon Valley (they are also active in other global innovation hubs) to scout new disruptive innovations that could help the bank on its journey to become "Number 1 for customer service, advocacy and trust." Senior RBS leaders often meet with innovation leaders and new technology players to discuss what can be expected in the coming years and which innovations hold most promise for the bank and for its customers. RBS has a range of approaches to support the flow of innovation back to their core business in the UK and to improve offerings and service to both enterprise and retail customers.

We have organized "learning journeys" for senior executive teams to expose them to the innovations most relevant to their current and future industry focus. Sometimes these are intact leadership teams from companies and sometimes they are delegations of executives from different companies, as when the consulting firm AT Kearney recently brought 40 of Germany's leading executives to the San Francisco Bay Area to explore how an innovation economy functions. These types of learning journeys are best designed with the specific objectives of each executive in mind and with the intent to stretch the thinking and loosen the mindset of what is possible and what should be in or out of the consideration set. They can have great value, especially at the outset of a process in which leaders want to get their own and their teams' minds engaged in the future and the innovations that are coming. But they are only a first step—like taking a vacation. Once you get home, you need everyday ways to cope with over-work or stress. Learning needs to be an everyday process, not a once-a-year trip to an innovation hub or center.

Innovation summits, like CES, E3, FiRe, SXSW, TechCrunch Disrupt, Web Summit, World Business Forum, Money 2020, WSJ Digital Live, and many others, provide great opportunities for immersion in new innovations and meeting those who are driv-ing them. We see innovation company leaders frequenting these events, giving keynotes, being panelists, holding private meetings and trawling booths to soak up knowledge of what is happening and what is coming.

More importantly, every day can be an innovation lesson if the leader is observant and has innovation top of mind: "I am at our competitor location, and they seem to have implemented a new xxxxx." "We are watching YouTube and just saw this really cool xxxxx." "I am with our staff in this location, and they just complained that our product is missing xxxxx, which makes us look bad." "I am trying our competitor's new product, and they simply have a better xxxxx." "I just saw this Kickstarter campaign on Facebook for someone who says they are going to build xxxxx. Really?"

This is the type of regular engagement in innovation that is most powerful. Every day asking the question, "What have I seen today that might improve my business or disrupt that of my com-petitors?" is an important way to keep innovation top of mind. This constant engagement and probing is along the lines of the mindset suggested by Andy Grove (1996) of Intel who famously said, "Success breeds complacency. Complacency breeds failure. Only the paranoid survive."

Leaders who are taking innovation seriously seek it out, bring it back, and share it in every meeting and more importantly, in real time with texts, emails, and other messages. Leaders drive their peers to take innovation seriously by their everyday demonstrations of passion for it.

"By Teaching, I'll Be Taught"

There is a lot of academic research that shows that when people teach, they learn. This can be within the company itself (which also has a powerful cultural impact that we will discuss later in Chapter 9) or outside. We see the leaders of the most innovative companies speaking about (thus teaching) innovation at conferences, summits, briefings, and so on.

For a senior leader to talk about a topic with knowledge, insight, and foresight requires a great deal of preparation, which itself ensures that the individual is becoming more capable. This is the practical way to ensure that very busy leaders continue to internalize the innovation messages and strategies of their companies. As Malcolm Gladwell (2008) put it, "Practice isn't the thing you do once you're good. It's the thing you do that makes you good."

We have already given the example of Mark Zuckerberg, who is actively out in the world engaging in discussions about future disruptive innovations. This extends to speaking and engaging in academic settings and among the next generation. Zuckerberg recently spoke at Alabama and North Carolina A&T, and is giving the Harvard commencement address as this book is published.

Teaching is also useful in that feedback can be direct and instantaneous if asked for. We see innovators sharing their thinking, then listening very carefully to the reactions and input from others. And more than once we have seen the next speech incorporating that feedback.

Our former partner at Monitor Group and Harvard Business

School Professor Michael Porter has been quoted as saying, "The best CEOs I know are teachers, and at the core of what they teach is strategy." In the transition to the Fifth Era, this is mostly innovation strategy.

Our Stanford classmate Allan Thygesen, President Americas at Google, manages Google's global small and mid-market advertiser business, which serves millions of customers and agencies worldwide. In his "spare" time Allan is a lecturer at Stanford Graduate School of Business where he teaches a course that examines the fundamental issues of creating a strategy for monetization and revenue growth within an organization. This type of direct teaching involvement has been shown to help the teacher remain current and engaged in new thinking and ideas.

In the next chapters, we will talk about how to get the broad employee base also engaged in the innovation challenge, thereby creating a culture of innovation. These moments in time in which leaders teach their people are like gold dust. They are often the most powerful moments for the broader organization as it begins to see what is important and valued in the culture of the company.

To put this into context, if your company has 10 directors and 10 senior executives, and if each of the directors holds a "teaching moment" once a month and each of the executives once a week for 50 of your people (some moments smaller, some larger, of course) on the topic of making your company innovative and agile, that means your team will touch 10 x 12 x 50 plus 10 x 52 x 50, which is 32,000 employees who could be directly spoken with (overlap of people would of course occur, but that means reinforcement of the message to those people).

Each of those direct points of contact can be very powerful. Digital communications, such as webinars, teleseminars, and live feeds, can engage a much wider audience in real time or after the fact, and then the message will be carried outwards and constantly reinforced.

Leaders who teach their people about innovation are unleashing a much more powerful force than those who simply tell their people what innovations to take to market.

More Diversity in Leadership Increases Creativity and Innovation

There is a building body of research that shows that when leadership teams are more diverse, they bring more ideas, perspectives and points of view, which can very positively impact the creativity and innovation of the combined team. This is true for leadership teams, boards of directors, and functional and divisional teams. Catalyst, the leading US nonprofit organization with a mission to accelerate progress for women through workplace inclusion, in summarizing the case for more women on executive teams and boards, shows through a synthesis of the academic and scientific research on gender diversity and its impact on performance that four important drivers are all positively impacted:

- Financial performance is improved.
- Companies are able to leverage a broader talent pool.
- The company better reflects the marketplace and creates a better reputation.
- Innovation is improved across the company.

Catalyst provides detailed research findings to support these points. As examples, using a sample of Fortune 500 corporate boards, Miller and del Carmen Triana (2009) found that innovation was positively and significantly correlated with board racial diversity, and marginally significantly correlated with board gender diversity. Studying 15 years of data on the management teams of S&P 1500 firms, Dezsö and Ross (2012) found that more women in top management improved the performance of firms that were heavily focused on innovation. Torchia, Calabrò, and

Huse (2011) found that reaching a critical mass of at least three women on a board has a positive impact on firm innovation, specifically "organizational innovation," which refers to the creation or adoption of a new idea or behavior.

Microsoft believes that as an innovation and technology-enabled company it must embrace all forms of diversity across the company. Microsoft has one of the more diverse boards of directors with three female board directors and a total of five out of eleven directors being either women or ethnic minorities. From the board, this requirement for diversity then ripples down into the company and its activities.

The innovation capacity of a company can be significantly increased by ensuring greater diversity – both at the most senior levels and throughout the company - to stimulate creativity and innovation in thinking and problem-solving.

A sclerotic or narrow mindset is the death of innovation.

The Role of the Chief Innovation Officer?

As companies strive to maintain relevance in light of the rapid implementation of the disruptive technologies that are the focus of this book, a new player has arrived at the executive table - the chief innovation officer. The chief innovation officer is responsible for looking at all products, services, and functions of the company, and ensuring that innovation is sufficiently represented and thought about in the strategic process of the company.

In some companies, the chief information officer or chief technology officer has been asked to broaden their scope to also become the chief innovation officer. In other companies, this is a new role that has been created with a singular focus on corporate innovation. In the most innovative and valuable companies in the world, the chief innovation officer is the CEO.

We see this latter model in place at the most innovative

companies: Apple (Steve Jobs now replaced by Tim Cook; Alphabet/Google (Larry Page and Sergey Brin); Amazon (Jeff Bezos); Facebook (Mark Zuckerberg); and Microsoft (Bill Gates, then Steve Ballmer, and now Satya Nadella).

This is not a coincidence. The CEO is always supposed to be the person who champions the vision, mission, and strategies of the company. For brand companies, the CEO has to be the brand champion. Now as we enter this period of disruption in every industry in every country, surely the CEO has to be the innovation champion and chief innovation officer.

In more established corporate settings and in companies where the CEO does not feel they have the capabilities and skills to lead innovation corporate-wide, they may decide to appoint a separate chief innovation officer. At least by adding this position to the senior executive team level, the company and its leadership are recognizing the critical importance for the future of the company. It is perhaps a better symbolic action than not having any member of the team focused on this most critical capability. However, it is better to embed the innovation mindset in every leadership member, and this is the approach at the most innovative companies.

In summary, the most innovative companies are all driving innovation top-down. Every member of the leadership team (board and executive) is expected to live and breathe innovation. The agendas of every major meeting include innovation topics throughout the year. The executive leadership team and board are all engaged in searching for, understanding, and sharing innovation ideas and insights, and many of them are teachers of others on these matters. Objectives, incentives, and so on are aligned to drive these behaviors; however, people are doing this because it is their passion—and those who can't get passionate or can't adjust to the new and changing future world are moving on or are being replaced by new players.

Chapter 8
Embed Innovation into
Strategies and Plans

Fortune brings in some boats that are not steered.

—William Shakespeare

With top-down leadership driving innovation into the company, we turn to the principal processes that drive corporate decision-making on a regular basis. Sometimes being in the right place at the right time is all we need, but usually more than a touch of luck is needed to turn an idea into success, and good planning seems to help a great deal.

There are very few corporate leaders who would trust fortune to bring their boat home. They are hired to steer it, which means they need a map, some navigation tools, and a good rudder. The corporate strategic planning process provides this direction setting.

Corporate Strategic Planning Approach

Most highly innovative companies give a great deal of thought to the creation and embedding of their innovation strategy into their corporate strategies and plans. In exploring this, we'll start by reviewing how the typical large company approaches strategic planning in terms of financial and resource allocation. Then we'll compare how innovative companies go about such strategic planning.

In most large corporations there is a well-defined approach to strategic planning for financial and resource allocation, orchestrated to ensure that all business units, geographies, and functional areas are aligned before the beginning of each financial year. In most North American companies where their financial year is aligned to the calendar year, these processes typically kick off with a corporate strategy review. In the late summer, the board of directors and the executive management team will sit together, frequently at an offsite, and review the high-level corporate strategy and the long-range strategic plan over a five-year or, in many industries, an even longer timeframe.

At the end of this examination and review, the board will approve the corporate strategy documents, which will be used by the executive team to drive alignment through the short-range financial plan for the coming year. In the next several months every business unit, geographical area, and functional area will be asked to ripple the key metrics and strategies of the long-term plan through their respective individual plans, and they will be asked to provide feedback as to both their future expectations and their ability to meet the financial goals and business goals that are being passed down to them.

The chief strategy officer and chief financial officer, working together, will then coordinate a process in which the roll-up of the business unit and geographic plans are synchronized to the functional plans to ensure that there is consistency and alignment between all elements of the company. The roll-up that results may need to be iterated, so that, for example, functional areas understand business unit expectations and adjust their plans accordingly, and vice versa.

By the last few months of the year, most large companies will have a reasonably comprehensive high-level corporate strategy, mid-term strategic roll-up, financial plans and functional plans to support them, and frequently their first cut of the next year's budget. The year finishes with the detailed creation of financial budgets and headcount requirements to support all of this planned activity.

Innovative Companies Align Strategies

This multidimensional process that we have just described is a substantial undertaking for large companies. However, a key differentiator of the most innovative companies is that they will also have something specifically called the innovation strategy and that innovation strategy will be integrated into all stages of the planning process. When we were with the Bay Area Council and Booz & Company, we co-authored a study in which we segmented the Global Innovation 1000, creating a separate group of those companies based in Silicon Valley and then comparing their results with all Global Innovation 1000 companies worldwide. Exhibit 19 shows how the Silicon Valley companies responded when compared to the average of all responses with regard to the degree to which there was alignment between the company's innovation strategy and its business strategy.

Exhibit 19

Innovation Strategy Alignment with Business Strategy

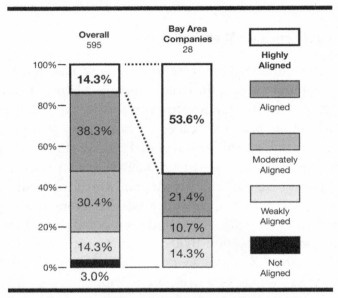

Sources: Bay Area Council Economic Institute, Booz & Company analysis

As can be seen, the Silicon Valley companies reported a much higher degree of alignment. Fully 75% of them said that their strategies were aligned (highly aligned or aligned). This compares with only 52.6% of the highest spending R&D companies in the world. In subsequent interviews, we found that large companies that only spend modestly on R&D have even lower levels of alignment and some do not have an innovation strategy at all.

Annual and Ongoing Alignment

The annual planning process is the place in which every aspect of innovation thinking and strategizing is channeled into the plans of the company. However, the most innovative companies continue the dialogue every day of the year. They do this both formally and informally.

Formally, we have seen innovative companies require every priority initiative to have a business unit or function leader as joint sponsor including a clear definition of the resources that the latter will bring to the innovation effort. If the business unit or functional leader is not prepared to co-sponsor the effort, it implies that there is not sufficient customer need or that other innovations are viewed as having higher priority.

We have also seen this formal alignment further reinforced with the use of innovation metrics and incentives. As just one example, at Barclays Global Investors (now Blackrock), we introduced as a key performance indicator the percentage of total revenue from products and services created in the last three years. This created a disciplined focus on new product and services innovations and launches across the company. Most notably, during this timeframe under the leadership of Pattie Dunn and Lee Kranefuss, BGI launched iShares, which is today the world's leading retail ETF provider with more than $1 trillion in assets under management.

Innovation Strategy Is Not Just Another Document

Importantly, the innovation strategy is not encapsulated in a separate document. Just as the human resources plan and the financial roll-up are lenses on the corporate, business unit, and product and services strategic plans, so the vast majority of the innovation plan is just another lens through which to view the priorities of the company.

Microsoft has not only implemented such a process across the company, but has also productized it and made it available to other companies. The Microsoft Innovation Management Framework is a structured approach to ensuring that the company goes through a series of discrete steps in its planning process around innovation strategy. Microsoft calls these stages Envision, Engage, Evolve, Evaluate, and Execute, and has technology tools to help its people through these parts of the development process.

As we shall see in Chapters 9 and 10, the completion of an effective innovation strategy also requires that additional questions be asked during the corporate strategic planning process. These questions are focused on surfacing realistic answers to guide the allocation of corporate resources and the need for external innovation strategies where the gaps can only be filled by others. For example:

- What innovation domains will we need to master given our corporate strategy?
- How do we prioritize across all of these innovation needs?
- Which of our internal resources are well-positioned to help us deliver?
- Conversely, what areas of innovation are we lacking?
- What external sources of innovation can help us where we are weak?
- What specific external innovation tactics can we use?

Traditional strategic planning processes do not ask these questions, so the overall direction of the corporation begins without sufficient consideration of the strategic choices, priorities, and capabilities that the company's future will require.

Tools for Developing Innovation Strategies

There are a number of methodologies that can be very helpful to leadership teams in surfacing potential areas of innovation that can either be used to create a competitive advantage or that need to be defended against. These methodologies are designed to help leaders manage in a future of uncertainty and are created to loosen and/or broaden the mindset of the leadership team, preparing them to consider alternative directions and identify needed areas of innovation and change.

While we will not fully describe these methodologies in this book, they include scenario planning, dynamic ecosystem management, industry-level wargaming, and disruptor analysis.

Our former partners, Peter Schwartz (1996, 2000), Eamonn Kelly (2005), and Peter Leyden (2000), have all written extensively on scenario planning and its use to help corporate leaders think more broadly about the future and about innovation in strategy and decision-making.

In 2005, we worked with Eamonn conducting scenario-planning exercises to help our client HP, one of the most innovative technology companies of the Industrial Era, come to terms with the rapidly changing world and its need for new forms of information technology products and services. Having explored future uncertainties and plausible scenarios, we were able to facilitate a large group of HP executives in defining the most likely future technology domains for HP, including blade computing, the cloud, distributed computing, mobility, cybersecurity, and so on. Kevin Kelly of *Wired* magazine was an external expert in that scenario-planning program and did a great job helping shift the mindset of our client by changing the framing of the discussion.

Meanwhile, our former colleague at AT Kearney, Paul Laudicina (2012), helped shape many executives' mindsets through his work on scenario planning and on building strategies for the future. As chairman emeritus of the consulting firm AT Kearney and current chairman of the Global Business Policy Council, Paul shares our view that it is critical for business leaders to think about the future in times of change and uncertainty, and to evaluate the robustness of their strategies in different future environments.

Ecosystem mapping, industry-level wargaming, and disruptor analysis serve as powerful tools for mapping likely directions of future industry development and directions from which new disruptive innovations and competitors may surface. At PayPal and StubHub we used these tools to map out these issues, surface priorities for the innovation strategy, and sequence which new innovations each respective company should bring to market.

Disciplined methodologies for building strategies in times of uncertainty are, however, few in number. Most large companies are very adept at defining plans for the businesses they already have in conditions they are already experiencing. In this time of change, it is much more difficult to decide where to focus with regard to new technologies and opportunities that may be surfacing and disrupting existing operations and competitive positions. Greater rewards will accrue to those who are able to plan ahead and be more clear-eyed about possible futures.

Risk Appetite and Tolerance for Failure

At this point in the book, we want to spend a moment on corporate risk tolerance. As Mark Zuckerberg, founder of Facebook, remarked, "The biggest risk is not taking any risk . . . In a world that is changing really quickly, the only strategy that is guaranteed to fail is not taking risks."

A great deal has been written about corporate risk tolerance and the difficulties associated with failing in large companies. While the entrepreneurial ecosystem takes failure as a given (50% to 70% of angel and venture capital-backed companies will return less than 100% of the capital invested), large companies can be unforgiving when strategies and plans go wrong. As a result, those who are responsible for creating plans with a high degree of risk tend to be less risk-seeking than external entrepreneurs. This is another reason that innovative companies tend to focus on exploiting external innovation, as we will see in Chapter 10.

Large companies are bad at celebrating failure and, as a result, are bad places to take risks unless they have created an innovation culture.

The most innovative companies handle this issue not by trying to create incentives to encourage risk tolerance but rather by creating a culture where everyone is focused on the customer and passionate about improving offerings to meet their needs. This brings a significant collateral benefit of greater risk tolerance. In an innovative culture, leaders will say, "I appreciate that you tried to do something fantastic for our customers, and we know you had their interests at heart," rather than, "You failed and your intent really does not make a difference in how I regard you." In Chapter 9 we discuss the creation of this risk-supporting culture.

Despite this observation, there is value in modifying planning requirements, approval processes, incentives, and project and personnel evaluation approaches to encourage risk-taking that supports key customer innovation priorities. It can't hurt to engineer in some risk tolerance and treat innovators differently from those who manage and drive established core businesses.

In summary, the most innovative companies are moving to a new corporate innovation approach in which the core processes of corporate decision-making and planning are brought into alignment with an innovation strategy that has been developed both in parallel and aligned with the other strategic plans of the company.

If your company has an innovation strategy that everyone understands and which is aligned with and embedded into the business strategies, it looks more like the most innovative companies. If it doesn't, your company surely has not yet begun the process of shifting to the new Fifth Era innovation approach.

Chapter 9
Build an Innovation Culture

Basic philosophy, spirit, and drive of an organization have far more to do with its relative achievements than do technological or economic resources, organizational structure, innovation, and timing.

—Marvin Bower

So far we have covered two aspects of the new corporate innovation approach. The first is that innovation is being driven top-down into the company by a passionate innovation-focused leadership team. Second, the core strategic processes of the company are ensuring that innovation is fully aligned with corporate and business strategy and that functional plans and processes echo this central place of innovation in the company.

Now we turn to the third element of the new corporate innovation approach—culture and the shared values of the company.

Innovative Companies Have Cultures That Support Innovation

We agree with Marvin Bower, the longtime leader of McKinsey & Company, when he emphasizes philosophy, spirit, and drive over everything else including technology and innovation. In large companies, a motivated and aligned culture can ensure great success. Conversely, seeds of greatness can go unwatered and die in cultures that are dry, barren, and unwelcoming. The best innovations in the world only flourish when a corporate culture supports and drives them forward.

The third element is the creation of a culture that supports innovation and in which every employee, from the top leadership to the functional, divisional and frontline staff, is passionate, spirited, and driven towards finding better and more innovative ways to serve customers. Such a culture ensures there is a high degree of alignment between the culture of the company and the innovation strategy.

In our work analyzing Global Innovation 1000 companies based in Silicon Valley we found that 73% of them say their culture supports their innovation strategy while only 51.5% of the highest spending Global Innovation 1000 companies could say the same. The Silicon Valley companies believe that their internal cultures support their innovation strategy and work hard to accomplish this goal.

Exhibit 20

Company Culture Alignment with Innovation Strategy

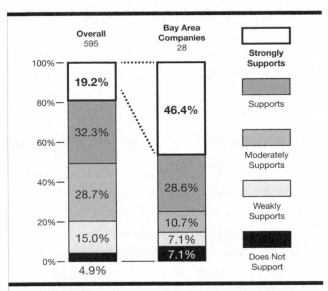

Sources: Bay Area Council Economic Institute, Booz & Company analysis

How do you build that supporting culture if you don't already have it?

One practical way to assess the degree to which the culture of the company supports its innovation strategy is simply to ask people at various levels whether or not they can describe the innovation strategy of their own company. In highly innovative companies, people several levels below the executive team, and sometimes all the way at the level of the frontline staff, can give a reasonably clear description of the innovation strategy. To use the example of Alphabet/Google, most employees can describe the Google mission, which is "to organize the world's information and make it universally accessible and useful." Similarly, at Facebook, most people can recite their mission, which is "to give people the power to share and make the world more open and connected." They may not recite these exact words verbatim, but they can articulate the core themes consistently.

In companies where the culture is less supportive of innovation, we find a much more rapid decay, in which very few people in the company, and sometimes even members of the CEO's executive team, are unable to describe the mission of the company with any degree of accuracy.

When we ask the follow-up question, "What is your innovation strategy?" or even, "What innovations do you think are most likely to help your company achieve its mission?" the employees at the most innovative companies can take a crack at answering while those at other companies usually cannot.

At Tesla, Elon Musk aligned the company around a mission to accelerate the world's transition to sustainable energy. If we go into the Tesla store at our local shopping mall in Corte Madera, California, and ask any of the salespeople who are selling Tesla S and X models what their company is passionate about, they give an answer along these lines: they love Tesla because it is making the world a cleaner place; plus, they love that their cars outperform any internal combustion-powered car on the market, including Bugatti, Ferrari, and Aston Martin.

When the company's leadership team is driving innovation from the top, the messages are flowing throughout the company all of the time, and the plans and policies of the company are aligned with the innovation strategies; then the culture begins to take on board those innovation priorities.

When the innovation mission and strategy is lacking, the culture does not know how best to support the innovation needed.

Who Gets to Innovate in Your Company?

Assuming the top-down messages have been heard and that people understand the philosophy and intent, companies are then confronted by a fundamental question as they try to build cultural support for innovation.

Who gets to be innovative?

The most innovative companies have found a way to create a spirit and drive for innovation while at the same time limiting the ability for most people to be innovative. Indeed, even the most innovative companies have very few innovators in their employee ranks.

To best illustrate this conundrum and the way out of it, let's revisit three questions from the short corporate innovation survey in Chapter 6.

Question 1: Should all employees be able to innovate the products and services that your company offers?

Almost every company in the world answers "no" to this question. The reality is that most employees in most companies are there to manufacture, market, distribute, sell, and service products and services that are given to them, and they have limited ability or responsibility to adjust those products and services in any way at all.

In some industries, such as banking and healthcare, any degree of flexibility to adjust key features of products and services, such as pricing and discounts, can lead to very serious negative ramifications from a regulatory, discriminatory, or other policy dimension. Even in companies where there is no negative consequence of treating some customers differently than others, it's typically the case that these fundamental levers are not given to the mass of employees at the company to adjust. As a result, in most companies, most employees do not have any role at all in innovating products and services.

This is also true in the most innovative companies.

The exception to the above is that in many cases employees are asked to provide ideas, input, and perspectives about new products and services. As an example, Amazon uses employee suggestion boxes on their internal website to gather employee suggestions for new innovations. In 2004 an Amazon software engineer named Charlie Ward famously suggested the idea of a free shipping service. This was the genesis for Prime, which is today one of Amazon's most important and most disruptive (to others) business offerings. However, these suggestion boxes, which are used in one way or another in most companies, tend not to be the drivers of innovation but are rather useful in gathering other types of employee input.

Innovation in most companies is not a broadly distributed responsibility.

Question 2: What percentage (X%) of your employees does have a mandate to innovate products and services in your company?

In most companies, X is less than 10%. In most companies, only a small portion of the total employee base has a mandate to change the fundamental aspects of the products and services being offered by the company, even in small, incremental ways. Disruptive changes are the responsibility of so small a number of people in most large companies as to be a rounding error.

Again, this is broadly true of the most innovative companies too. In some industries, there is a higher percentage of the workforce involved in the innovation process, for example, in the biotechnology industry and the software industry. In other industries, such as retailing, it is a tiny percentage of the population. But the point is always valid: in all companies, the vast majority of people are not going to be personally involved in innovating your offerings.

Question 3: What does innovation as a shared value mean to the rest of your people, your total population less the proportion X that you described in question 2?

Taken together, these three questions set up the most important question for companies to consider as they think about how to build a culture of innovation as part of their new innovation approach.

The CEO and leadership team need to develop a corporate-wide spirit and drive that will support a culture of innovation while not allowing most employees to innovate themselves.

The importance of this is fundamental because the culture of innovation of the company has to support the innovation strategy for it to be deployed company-wide, and the people of the company will ultimately need to implement innovations as they are surfaced and taken to market.

This then leads us to the important question: how do the most innovative companies solve this conundrum?

Key Cultural Attributes That Support Innovation

In Exhibit 21, we show the results of a survey of the most innovative companies in which we asked them, "What are the key cultural attributes that you believe are most important in supporting your innovation approach?"

Exhibit 21

Key Cultural Attributes That Support Innovation

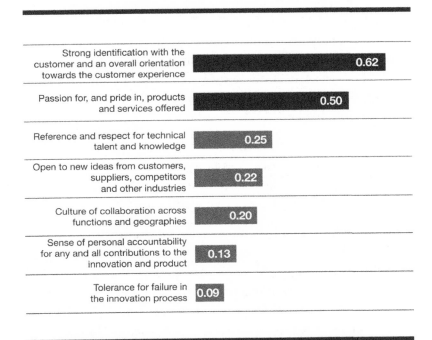

Note: Please force-rank the following cultural attributes in order of the relative level of importance to your company and the degree of prevalence. Rank the most important 1st , the next most important 2nd and so on.
— Responses above reflect the recoded means, that is, responses

Importantly, the first two attributes stand out as being much more important than the others. The most innovative companies say that the cultural attributes that drive innovation are:

1. A strong identification with the customer and an overall orientation towards the customer experience (and constantly making sure it is competitive and getting better)
2. A passion for and pride in the products and services

being offered by the company (including ensuring that they are leading edge and fully competitive with those of other players in the industry)

Interestingly, our good friend Michael Dunn's firm Prophet publishes an annual brand relevance index that assesses those brands that are seen as being most relevant to their lives by customers globally. The dimensions that appear to be most important in driving this brand relevance are:

1. Customer obsession
2. Ruthless pragmatism
3. Pervasive innovation
4. Distinctive inspiration

In 2016, the ranking of the most relevant brands to US consumers was: 1) Apple, 2) Amazon, 3) Android (Alphabet/Google), 4) Netflix, and 5) Google (Alphabet/Google).

In the UK, the ranking was 1) Apple, 2) Google (Alphabet/Google), 3) Amazon, 4) PlayStation (Sony), and 5) Netflix.

In Germany it was 1) Amazon, 2) Apple, 3) Google (Alphabet/Google), 4) Lego, and 5) Netflix.

This and other studies confirm that an obsessive focus on customer needs and a pride in the products and services of the company are not only cultural attributes that support innovation but also are drivers of ensuring brand relevancy with customers. These two elements are closely connected and are the keys to the conundrum.

Obsessed about Customer Needs

The key to unlocking the culture of innovation conundrum is to begin with the customer.

Innovative companies create a culture in which everyone,

regardless of their mandate to innovate, is tasked with understanding the customer and seeking ways for the company to do a better job in serving the customer, both with today's products and services and in the future. One of the executives we interviewed while working on the Booz & Company Innovation Global 1000 said it very well. Agilent CTO Darlene Solomon noted: "There's a very strong innovation culture throughout the company and a culture of teamwork, and Agilent really encourages that. Innovation is not just R&D here. We've really tried to make clear that it's about everybody questioning the status quo and looking to do something better than what's been done before."

The goal is to make everyone in the company into a "need seeker." They all have a deep passion for understanding the needs of each customer and the degree to which they are currently met and unmet by the company and by its competitors. One hundred percent of the organization needs to hold this mindset. The "spirit" of the company is that it is there to serve the customer, and everyone should and must understand what they want and what they are currently getting.

Exhibit 22 provides a simple schematic of the parts of this dynamic that fuel the culture of innovation.

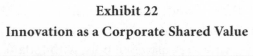

Exhibit 22

Innovation as a Corporate Shared Value

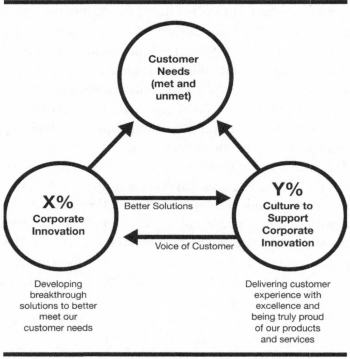

Source: Fifth Era, LLC

At Apple, this is woven deeply into their culture. A former Fifth Era intern had previously worked at an Apple store in Marin County, California, before attending college, to double major in computer science and mathematics. Highly innovative in his mindset and a member of Generation C, he quickly found that in an Apple store the focus is entirely on the customer and identifying their needs, making sure they understand the options that Apple can provide, and then helping them to make their own choices regarding which Apple products to take home. An Apple store swarms with Apple employees who are trying their very best to serve the customer. And there is enormous pride among the Apple people for their company and its products and services. In fact, getting an internship or job at an Apple store is a substantial undertaking itself with many more people being turned away than accepted. Apple people like to say that it is easier to get into Stanford than to get a job at Apple. This may or may not be true, but there is a feeling of privilege to work there and to have the opportunity to serve customers and fulfill the Apple mission.

Another Booz interviewee, Fred Palensky, executive vice president of research and development and CTO at 3M, explained, "Our goal is to get the voice of the customer all the way back to the basic research level and the product development level, to make sure our technical people actually see how their technologies work in various market conditions."

One other way that the most innovative companies ensure that their frontline is able to have a voice in the development process is to allow them early access to new products and services before they are made final so that they can use them and point out changes that they believe customers will find beneficial. Aliza Knox who has worked as a senior executive at Google, Twitter, and now Unlocked puts it this way, "Companies really seeking to drive innovation make sure all of their employees have access to company products, especially new versions in beta. This way employees can test and give feedback, even if they are in back office functions. This tends to be called 'eating your own dogfood' and enables everyone to participate as a customer."

This passion for getting to the root of customer needs, met and unmet, is a hallmark of companies that have built strong innovation cultures.

Corporate Innovators

In the most innovative companies, those small number of people who have been given a mandate to innovate are then tasked to constantly track customer needs and look over the horizon to try and predict what new solutions may be forthcoming driven by innovations from within or from outside the industry. They do this by talking to customers themselves, tracking competitors, scanning the broader environment, and most importantly from listening to the rest of their own organization.

Secondly, they are tasked with constantly coming up with better solutions to enable the organization to better serve customer needs.

Amazon founder and CEO Jeff Bezos described the role of his corporate innovation teams very well when he stated, "We're a company of builders. Of pioneers. It's our job to make bold bets, and we get our energy from investing on behalf of customers." A good example of this in action is Amazon Prime Now. Amazon customers had expressed a desire for faster deliveries ever since the company was first founded. Taken to an extreme, Amazon decided to see what the fastest possible delivery time might be. Within 111 days they created and launched a pilot, first in Manhattan and now in several cities in the US and in London, UK, whereby customers can place an order and receive delivery of selected goods within an hour. Two-hour delivery is free and one-hour delivery is $7.99 in the US.

Here in Silicon Valley, we see this passion for finding better solutions also being demonstrated by the scouting teams from many international companies. Companies as diverse as HTC from Taiwan, Huawei from China, Orange from France, RBS from the UK, Samsung from Korea, Axel Springer from Germany, and so forth, have sent scouting teams to prowl through the ecosystem looking for great ideas and innovations to deploy on behalf of their customers.

The Rest of the Organization

For the rest of the organization, two roles are emphasized. The first is to be the eyes and ears of the organization, and the second is to be the voice of the customer.

Eyes and Ears
Being the eyes and ears of the organization means to be constantly aware of how customer needs are being met and also constantly tracking the degree to which the company is not competitive with the offerings of competitors, as well as identifying those times when competitors are making adjustments to products and services. In most companies, almost 100% of the customer and competitor touchpoints are owned by those people who are not allowed to innovate themselves. Making sure that those touchpoints are made "active" such that customer needs and concerns are constantly surfaced and tracked is the first way to ensure that innovation needs are defined and prioritized.

Voice of the Customer
The second role for the rest of the organization is to be the voice of the customer, feeding into the corporate innovation teams and into their innovation strategies and agendas. This ensures that the company is delivering its customer experience with excellence and that everyone can be truly proud of the company's products and services.

This can be very powerful. As Eckhart Tolle put it, "The power for creating a better future is contained in the present moment: you create a good future by creating a good present."

Making sure the customer is happy today gives you the opportunity to attempt to make them happy tomorrow.

When senior leaders meet with frontline staff, it is very important to see how the staff behave around this issue of the voice of the customer. In the most innovative companies, they are vocal, forceful, and even difficult in ensuring that their leaders understand what the customers want and what's not happening, and they are especially vocal in sharing their fears if they see competitive products "eating their lunch" with their customers. They are proud of their company and its offerings, and they become very anxious if they see their pride misplaced or threatened.

At Gap, we lived this in practice. The then CEO Mickey Drexler, who is today CEO of J. Crew and was a board director of Apple for 16 years, would visit the stores every week and expected every executive in the company to do the same on a regular basis. Every Gap employee at that time was encouraged to speak out regarding any customer issue, directly to Mickey or to any other Gap Inc. executive. While a good amount of effort went into finding out why things might not be working in the field as designed in headquarters, an equal number of issues raised were valuable insights into the customer and how they were feeling about Gap versus its competitors. Today, we can't enter a retail store environment without seeing it through those detail- and customer-oriented eyes that we developed in those years at Gap.

Interestingly, while Mickey was on the board of Apple, Steve Jobs was on the board of Gap. Leading the Gap strategy and business development team in that timeframe was very instructive. Mickey was asked by Steve to give perspective on issues like the colors of the initial Apple Mac (before then, all computers were gray, black, or tan). Steve was asked to come and share his belief in customer focus at the Gap annual leadership conference in 2000. The themes in this section could have been written by either Mickey or Steve since both lived them every day. When Apple eventually launched its retail stores (today probably the most productive retail space in the world), it was humbling to see how Steve and his team took the very best ideas from Gap retail stores and then fine-tuned them to create a first in the consumer electronics space: a truly customer-centric retail experience in which the frontline staff is actively listening to every customer all of the time.

Conversely, in companies that lack this spirit and drive for innovation, we see the frontline staff passive, not vocal, and sometimes fearful of sharing what they know to be true. They have lost the passion, spirit, and drive that Marvin Bower described, and they don't have a culture of continuous improvement and innovation, nor do they feel proud to work for the company since they see it falling short in meeting customer needs.

In the most innovative companies, the rallying cry of serving customers is the key to making sure that both those with a mandate to innovate and those without that mandate come together in a shared passion for driving innovations from their company and into the customers' hands.

It also creates a spirit and drive for making every product and service fully competitive or superior to others in the market. The organization becomes proud of its offerings once it can see that they meet customer needs better than others. And conversely, this desire to be proud creates enormous urgency to fix things when it becomes clear that the pride is misplaced because the company has fallen or is falling behind competitors and/or customers are not happy.

Some technology companies are beginning to use new tools to make sure that the organization can speak in real time to their leadership as they see issues arising. At Eventbrite, founders Julia and Kevin Hartz implemented an internal Net Promoter Score to judge whether they are building a company that has a culture that everyone is proud of and then added tools like a chat app called Slack that connects people with others they need to do their jobs effectively and in-depth quarterly surveys with the polling tool Culture Pulse. Tools like these can connect the employees with the leadership of a company and enable real-time communication concerning issues as soon as they are identified.

Before we leave the issue of corporate culture, let's briefly discuss organization structure. While organization is not just structure, structure can play an important role. Sidebar 5:

Concerning Organizational Structure provides some perspective on this issue.

Sidebar 5: Concerning Organizational Structure

Organizational structure is very company-specific, and while important in making a company effective, it is hard to make generalizations about how to organize in order to optimize innovation as part of the corporate innovation approach. The most innovative companies appear to use somewhat different organizational structures for driving their innovation activities.

It is useful to take a look at Exhibit 23, which provides some thought starters for large multi-business and multi-geography corporations that may be debating the structural issue.

Exhibit 23
Corporate Innovation Conceptual Organizational Structure

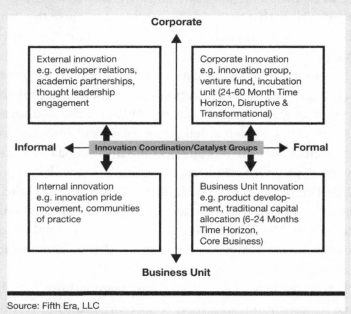

Source: Fifth Era, LLC

In Exhibit 23, the innovation challenge is arrayed in a matrix defined by the center of gravity of each activity. Is it more at the corporate center or more decentralized to the business units? And in the other dimension, is the activity a formal innovation activity, or is it more informal?

Business Unit Innovation. In the bottom right, business unit innovation is a formal, decentralized body of innovation activities often focused on "incremental" innovations to close competitive gaps in better meeting customers' needs and/or ensuring that today's products continue to improve. The time horizons tend to be shorter (in many industries this type of innovation is organized around a 6- to 24-month time horizon), and the innovations are very focused on today's core business(es).

Corporate Center Innovation. In the top right are the centralized corporate innovation efforts. Longer term in nature (often 24 to 60 months or longer), the emphasis is on disruptive and transformational innovations rather than more incremental ones that are the focus of the business unit innovation efforts. This group of activities may include corporate venture funds, incubation units, and other tools described in Chapter 11.

Internal Innovation. In the bottom left are internal innovation efforts focused on creating the culture of innovation that was the focus of this section: innovation pride movements, communities of practices within the company, voice of the customer efforts, and so on, all activities focused on creating the internal passion for innovation that is so important.

External Innovation. In the top left are those activities that focus on external sources of innovation for the company to tap into. These are described more fully in the next two chapters (10 and 11).

Innovation Coordination/Catalyst Groups. Finally, in the center is a small group tasked with coordinating and prioritizing across all of the other activities. In companies where there is a chief innovation officer, this may be that person and a small central staff. In other companies, this is the role of the CEO and their senior executive leadership team with some staff support.

We offer this to be thought-provoking, not as a specific recommendation as part of the new corporate innovation approach that is championed in this book. Not only is organizational structure very company-specific, but there is so much change as we usher in the Fifth Era that entirely new approaches to corporate organization and structure are beginning to surface.

As an example of just how different organizational structure can look in a truly innovative company, consider Alphabet/Google. Here Larry Page, Sergey Brin, and Eric Schmidt have broken the company into two with the Google part focused on today's products and services—with constant innovation still as a theme—and Alphabet being the part of the company focused on future disruptive opportunities for the corporation. As Larry Page writes, "Sergey and I are seriously in the business of starting new things. Alphabet will also include our X lab, which incubates new efforts like Wing, our drone delivery effort. We are also stoked about growing our investment arms, Ventures and Capital, as part of this new structure." (We will discuss X lab and Ventures and Capital later in Chapter 11 The External Innovation Toolkit). While a structural division of a company into two halves organized around innovation may be a little extreme, it demonstrates very well how when a company makes innovation its raison d'être, it leads to a passion, drive, and spirit, which take the company in new and sometimes unexpected directions.

We began this chapter by quoting Marvin Bower and his belief that a passionate, spirited, and driven organization are the most important attributes of all. We showed that in the context of corporate innovation, this means developing a culture that supports innovation across the entire company. This means solving the conundrum that most people do not have a mandate to innovate, so their engagement and support needs to be captured in some other way. The key to unlocking this conundrum is to use the customer experience to drive a passion for innovation. Most people can become the eyes and ears of the organization in interacting with customers and the voice of the customer in bringing the insights back to bear on the innovation efforts. While only a few have the mandate to innovate, they are supported and cheered on by the many and, ultimately, by the customer.

Let us close this chapter with another quote. This time from another management theorist, Gary Hamel, in which he underscores the importance of innovation in driving long-term customer loyalty: "Most of us understand that innovation is enormously important. It's the only insurance against irrelevance. It's the only guarantee of long-term customer loyalty. It's the only strategy for outperforming a dismal economy."

Chapter 10
Exploit External Innovation

Human beings, who are almost unique in having the ability to learn from the experience of others, are also remarkable for their apparent disinclination to do so.

—Douglas Adams

The final element that makes up the new approach to innovation is a refocusing of innovation activities to ensure that there is an appropriate mix of external versus internal effort. The most innovative companies are fully exploiting innovations being generated outside their own organization rather than relying on their own far more limited capability.

Where Will Innovations Come From?

In order to illustrate the importance of this change, let's start by reviewing answers to some more of the questions posed in the Corporate Innovation Survey in Chapter 6.

Over the next decade where will the most important innovations in your industry come from?

       a. Your company
       b. Your industry
       c. Outside your industry

Consistently we find that almost no one who responds to this question selects option A, that the most important innovations in their industry will come from their own company. Almost without exception respondents to this question split roughly 50-50 between those who believe the most important innovations will come from other players within their industry, Option B, or will come entirely from outside their industry, Option C.

The importance of this question is self-explanatory: most innovations that need to be scouted, tracked, and eventually adopted will be coming from outside the four walls of your own company.

Where Are Your Innovation Resources Focused?

The next question is "What percent of your innovation spend is internal versus external—people and capital combined?"

This question does vary significantly across companies. However, in many industries respondents say that as much as 90% of the people and capital resources focused on innovation are being spent internally. In some industries, this number may be in the range of 60% to 70%, but rarely do respondents answer that less than half of the capital and resources of their innovation activities are being spent internally.

If you answered that a majority of your company's innovation resources are spent externally rather than internally (and assuming you are a large corporation), then you are in the minority and look much more like the most innovative companies that have also pivoted to relying more heavily on the world's innovators.

Are You Looking Beyond Your Industry?

The final question in this section of the survey is "What percent of your innovation spend focuses beyond your industry?"

This final question almost always is answered in the diminutive. Almost all respondents answer that very little, typically 10%

or less, of the innovation spend of their companies is looking beyond the current confines of their industry.

Most companies define their relevant innovation consideration set within their current industry definition and within the current competitive set. It takes a rare leader to put energy into contemplating the innovations of industries and competitors that have no current overlap with their own company's offerings.

Fundamental Opportunity vs. Resource Mismatch

The combination of these three questions provides the fundamental challenge for adjusting the fourth element of the corporate innovation approach. In most companies and in most industries people agree that the most important innovations of the coming future will come from other players in their industry or from outside their industry from other disruptive players.

Conversely, most large companies today still spend most of their capital and people resources on internal innovation, and most companies spend a diminutive portion of those resources looking beyond their industry. This is a fundamental resource mismatch and opportunity.

The challenge of the coming years is to realign the people and capital resources that are tasked with innovation, shifting the majority of them to focus on sources of external innovations and greatly increase the proportion that is being spent on scouting, tracking, and adopting innovations arising from beyond today's industry definition.

Reorienting towards External Innovation

In order to reorient towards external innovation, there are two challenges for most large companies. The first is to create their external innovation strategy leveraging the breadth of external innovation tools which we describe more fully in Chapter 11. The second is to greatly scale back the current internal innovation capability. It is the latter that tends to make it hard to do the former.

In developing the external innovation strategy it is useful to structure the issues in the sequence outlined in Sidebar 6: What Are the External Innovation Priorities?

Sidebar 6: What Are the External Innovation Priorities?

1. The first question is: "What are the innovation priorities for the company and what 'innovation domains' need to be covered by the internal and external innovation strategies?"

- We assume that the company now has a clear innovation strategy that is fully aligned with the corporate and business strategies and is supported by the culture of the company.

- This strategy should have captured and influenced the roll-up of the innovation priorities of the business units as they seek to meet the current and future needs of target customers in a competitive setting.

- It should also include areas of potential disruptive innovation that need to be explored because they provide potential to create economic value for the company either within the existing core businesses or in proximate areas that may be added to the focus on the company.

- These innovation priorities can often be grouped into "innovation domains," which are areas of research, technology development, and so on.

This provides the sum of innovation priorities and domains that need to be covered by the combination of the internal and external innovation activities.

2. The second question is: "Where can the internal teams best contribute?"

What innovations are already in the pipeline and portfolio?

- In which innovation domains are the internal research and development teams strongest?

- Comparing these strengths with the innovation priorities, what is our thinking on how best to leverage the internal resources?

At this stage, no decision is being made to leverage the internal resources; this is an assessment concerning where they can potentially add the most value and be successful.

3. The third question is: "What is the best way to leverage external innovation resources?"

For those innovation domains that are critical to the innovation priorities of the company but where the skills and capabilities do not exist in-house or are insufficiently represented, the next step is to find and assess external sources that can be leveraged:

- Where is each of the needed innovation domains best represented in the external environment, and which researchers, laboratories, companies, think tanks, etc., have the requisite expertise in these areas?

- To which of these domains does the company already have access, and where will it need to forge new partnerships, alliances, or other structures for collaboration?

- Where would the external sources of innovation most likely do a better job than the company's own internal capability?

4. The fourth question is: "Which external innovation tools should we prioritize?"

Having identified the most appropriate external centers of technology or sources of insight, the innovation leader must then determine which external innovation tools to focus on. This will involve a combination of the executive team's stance regarding risk—cost tradeoffs and the specific characteristics of the external sources of innovation. Key questions include the following:

- Which set of external innovation tools will provide the best access to the needed innovation domains?

- Which of the tools are already prototyped at the company, and how can they be scaled to the requisite levels to ensure success?

- What is the company's risk-cost trade-off tolerance in creating the needed tools?

- How does its risk tolerance affect the use of each external innovation tool and its relative weight in the overall external innovation strategy?

5. The final question is: "What skills, organizational resources, financial resources, governance processes, performance measurement systems and other elements, and activities are needed to implement a successful external innovation strategy?"

Setting up an external innovation program requires the development of the proper set of internal capabilities to ensure that the company is viewed by external innovation players as an attractive partner; to raise the likelihood of success of the external innovation activities; and to prepare the company to exploit those new technologies and products once they are ready to be brought in-house for launch and roll-out. Key questions include the following:

- What assets, capabilities, and resources does the company as a whole already possess to help make external innovation tools and efforts successful?

- What capabilities are needed to ensure that the company is viewed by external parties as a preferred partner as it expands its external innovation strategy?

- Which elements of the company's current internal innovation activities are likely to hamper its external innovation efforts, making it more difficult to integrate those efforts into the company?

- What changes to the company's operating model—including goals, strategies, roles and responsibilities, processes, and governance model— will be necessary to ensure that an expanded external innovation strategy operates successfully?

The chief innovation officer (whoever plays this role in the company) now has to develop the comprehensive business plan that outlines the focus of external innovation activities, requests funding, proposes resource allocations, and then provides projections of the expected benefits of the new capability for the growth trajectory of the company. The plan must take into account the implications for funding, governance, the organization, and performance management and incentives.

Funding the External Innovation Strategy

- How much capital (and/or what percentage of operating expenses) will be needed?

- How many external innovation tools must be supported, and what level of funding and allocations will be needed to support each one?

- What are the expectations for self-funding the capability at some point (as opposed to a purely strategic investment)?

Governance

- What new decision authorities will be needed across the organization?

- What new decision-making processes must be put in place?

The Organization

- Where should the external innovation capability be located within the broader innovation organization?

- How should the external innovation capability be organized?

- What mix of current staff and new hires will be needed?

- What competency profiles are needed for a successful external innovation program?

- How should compensation and incentives be structured (including, in some cases, upside sharing)?

Performance Metrics and Incentives

- What metrics and key performance indicators will be needed to track the new capability's performance?

- How should revenue and earnings targets and goals be structured?

- Can a corrective action feedback loop be put in place to continually improve performance?

> - What is a reasonable time horizon for measuring success (quarterly targets, annual goals, a five-year plan)?
>
> This is a modified version of the questions outlined in our earlier paper (Le Merle & Campbell, 2009), which is included in the references.

As companies form a strategy and a business plan for an external innovation capability, they must constantly remind themselves and their internal innovation organization that the whole point of the external innovation exercise is to access external innovators that are fast-moving, lean, and very loosely structured. Care must be taken not to slow down or stifle the external innovation program by layering on too much "big company thinking and process." At the same time, no company can reap the benefits of an external innovation strategy without careful consideration of how to make use of the linkages, points of integration, and critical assets of the larger firm that can help the external innovation strategy succeed.

Scaling Back Internal Innovation

Our former partner Michael Porter is famous for saying that corporate strategy is as much about deciding what not to do as what to do. So it goes in innovation too. Once the external innovation strategy has been defined and resourced, there is a need to make choices about what no longer to do internally.

This is often the hardest part of the journey. For example, in the pharmaceutical industry, there have been massive changes in innovation activities over the last decade. Historically, the pharmaceutical giants, like GlaxoSmithKline, Merck, and Pfizer, owned the largest research and development organizations in the world. They spent billions of dollars and employed tens of thousands of scientists within their four walls. Then the Biotechnology Revolution began and increasingly the pharmaceutical giants saw their internal innovation efforts yielding ever less in the way of new drugs and revenue, and conversely, new biotechnology leaders like Amgen, Chiron, Genentech, and Gilead surfaced. We worked at all four of these, as well as others, and were always impressed how masters in the new life sciences technologies, these smaller, more agile innovators were able to out-innovate much larger players. The results were several: the pharmaceutical giants partnered, joint ventured, and acquired the more innovative life sciences companies; they refocused their own efforts increasingly on sourcing new solutions through external innovation; and they greatly scaled back their own internal innovation efforts. Pfizer alone saved billions of dollars by taking scaling-back actions while almost every other pharmaceutical major has done the same, with many, such as Sanofi and GlaxoSmithKline, continuing to reduce internal efforts as recently as 2015.

In summary, the most innovative companies have already embraced the thought that they cannot be the drivers of innovation themselves, that there is no monopoly on innovation either within their company or within their industry, and as a result they have realigned their resources, people, and capital to spend much more of it on external innovation both within the confines of their industry and by keeping a keen eye on the potentially disruptive innovations surfacing outside the industry.

In Chapter 11 of this book, we will describe a comprehensive external innovation toolkit that represents all of the specific tactics that a large company can use to engage more in external innovation and which are being used by the most innovative companies.

Chapter 11
The External Innovation Toolkit

The mechanic that would perfect his work must first sharpen his tools.

—Confucius

Chapter 10 of this book briefly profiled the various ways that large companies can leverage external innovation. In this chapter, we take a deeper look at the specific tactics or "tools" that the most innovative companies are using to access external innovation. This chapter reviews the "external innovation toolkit" and is intended to build your knowledge of the breadth of external innovation choices and some of their respective pros and cons and who they are best suited to. While undeniably not comprehensive of every possible way for companies to play in external innovation, the following list of 17 tools covers most of the common approaches being leveraged by the most innovative companies.

Innovation leaders consistently demonstrate two characteristics in their use of the external innovation toolkit. The first characteristic is the degree to which they use the 17 tools. The most innovative companies use many or all of these tools on a scale and scope that is a magnitude greater than most large corporations. Secondly, the way in which they focus their external innovation strategy against their own innovation priorities is striking. This alignment creates sharp focus but also requires a great deal of management and constant tuning up of the use of each tool to ensure it continues to perform in the ways required to drive the company's objectives.

The external innovation toolkit we outline in this chapter covers 17 tools as follows:

We describe five external innovation tools focused on the academic community, researchers, and key opinion leaders:

1. Grants and Scholarships
2. Innovator Networks
3. Key Opinion Leader Networks
4. External Advisory Boards
5. Joint/Collaborative Research and Development Agreements

Three further external innovation tools are focused on the developer community and technology entrepreneurs with companies in their very first stages of formation:

6. Developer Certification and Support Programs
7. Third Party Incubators and Accelerators
8. Corporate Incubators and Accelerators

Four external innovation tools are investment-oriented, enabling companies to become direct and indirect investors in early-stage ventures as well as providing access to promising new innovations as they gain traction:

9. Crowdfunding Investments
10. Angel Co-Investment Fund LP Positions
11. Venture Capital LP Positions
12. Corporate Venture Programs

Five external innovation tools are focused on providing access to promising companies and their innovations by enabling licensing agreements, go-to-market partnerships, joint ventures, and acquisitions:

1. Venture Exchanges
2. In-Licensing Programs

3. Go-to-Market Partnerships
4. Joint Venture Programs
5. Acquisition Programs

This chapter briefly describes each of these tools, provides some examples of companies leveraging each, and then gives a brief assessment along the following three criteria:

- Risk of failure
- Cost to play
- Difficulty of implementation

Combined with the thought process outlined in Chapter 10, this should enable you to begin to create an external innovation strategy for your company.

The first five external innovation tools focus on the academic community, researchers, and key opinion leaders. Since in most cases, companies have not yet been formed around the innovations in development, and investment capital is not involved, the cost of playing is relatively low. The exception to this is where major financial support is given to sponsor or support a center of research, which can become a very costly undertaking. Most of these tools are also relatively easy to initiate and support on an ongoing basis.

1. Grants and Scholarships

Given that the locus of much research continues to be in academic centers of learning and higher education, there are a number of strategies that can be a part of the new corporate innovation approach that explicitly leverage the scientists and researchers in these institutions. Large companies can formally ally themselves with centers of research by providing funding at the institution level (also see joint research and development agreements below), at the faculty or department level, or at the level of support for specific professors, researchers, and teams. This support can come in the form of endowments, sponsorships, grants, and scholarships. By doing this, companies can gain access to the thinking and perspectives and, to some extent, the scientific breakthroughs of the researchers with whom they have allied. In some cases, this access is formalized in terms of joint development and partnership agreements. In other cases, it occurs through informal dialogue and interaction and collaboration.

One example from one of the most innovative companies is the Amazon Catalyst program created with the University of Washington. The program is open to all University of Washington students, faculty, and staff at the Seattle, Bothell, and Tacoma campuses, and proposals are selected in any field, including the humanities, engineering, the sciences, and the arts. Winners receive $100,000 and join a community of innovators—Amazon Catalyst Fellows—who share a passion for building solutions to real-world problems.

A second example is the Microsoft healthcare awards. Here Microsoft accepts nominations from a qualifying healthcare, pharmaceutical, biotechnology, clinical resource, or medical device organization worldwide, which has developed and implemented a solution independently or working with a technology solution partner, as long as the solution is in full implementation within an organization for at least 30 days and is based on the latest Microsoft technologies. In this case, the "winners" receive the honor of being selected as a proven and valuable product as well as support in marketing their solution, but there is no monetary reward.

These types of relationships with academic centers of research and external innovators can be built into networks by the careful selection of a family of institutions that are focusing on the areas of disruptive innovation and technology that the corporation is interested in gaining access to and by outreach to selected innovator communities. The most innovative companies make even sharper use of this tool by tracking and engaging at the researcher level. This requires a great deal of time and energy since tracking the specific research focus of individual scientists can become a massive task in many fields. However, within most fields, there are well-known researchers who are driving the frontiers of the field, and those within the field usually have visibility into these people. Advisory boards can be helpful in finding them (see below).

There are two further challenges with optimizing the use of this tool. The first is that over time most leading researchers in a field will already have entered the radar screens of competing players and they may already have established relationships, which limit their ability to accept support from another corporation. To combat this, it can make sense to track up-and-coming researchers including those pushing frontiers within the teams and laboratories of more established scientists. Once these individuals are engaged in a discussion by a supportive sponsor, they may be very interested in creating their own programs and efforts.

The second challenge with this tool is to ensure that it is used dynamically. Areas of disruptive innovation can change quickly, and new researchers may need to be added as the areas of interest change while those who have been backed in the past may lose their relevance. We have seen many cases in which inertia continues a portfolio of grants and scholarships even when the company's areas of interest are no longer the focus of the scientists concerned.

Most companies will find it beneficial to include some level of this tool into their overall external innovation strategy.

Risk	High
Cost	Low
Implementability	Easier

2. Innovation Networks

Innovation networks are a mechanism for gaining access to a large number of individuals with relevant expertise, research focus, or understanding outside the context of whatever formal working settings and relationships they may reside within. Innovation networks are often sponsored by government and industry players to stimulate collaborative work between scientists. For example, in the healthcare arena, collaborative innovation networks are formed from time to time to address specific health-related challenges, including contagious outbreaks and diseases where scientists need to work rapidly together to create new solutions. Examples of outbreaks that resulted in such collaborative networks include SARS, Ebola, etc.

These innovation networks can be open, where a variety of companies may collaborate together for shared purposes, or they may be closed, in which case they are essentially created by and run by one corporation only.

In the case of open networks, private sector players can join both to share their own insights and to gain access to others. While this is easier than forming a closed innovation network because it does not require any need to sponsor and manage the other participants in the network, it can be harder to ensure proprietary access and competitive advantage. The network is open, and insights will be broadly shared.

Closed, proprietary networks can be created when a company identifies the thought leaders within the domains of technology and innovation that they're focused on. By inviting those individuals to participate in the company's privately owned and operated innovation network, a company can hope to gain insights and access to important innovations while they're being developed.

Typically, innovation networks provide multiple forms of

benefit to the individuals participating. On the one hand, there may be some compensation for participation. There is the expectation that the individuals will learn from the experience at the same time as they give insights into the network, and sometimes there's the opportunity for the network members to formally participate in collaborative innovation or paid opportunities being driven by the corporation.

As the Internet and connected technologies have improved, so the effectiveness of these innovation networks has too. Today corporate sponsors manage very large global innovation networks with sophisticated relationship management software, posting needs and allowing researchers to bid to take on work, using collaborative technologies to share data, insights, and findings, and even running collaborative research with many scientists working on an issue simultaneously. We have also seen the creative use of incentives ranging from prizes for winners in innovation competitions, to auction tools to manage multiple bidding by innovation network members and so on.

The most innovative companies are building innovation networks, and we think technology-enabled versions are certainly an essential tool of the future for tapping into external innovators.

Risk	High
Cost	Low
Implementability	Easier

3. Key Opinion Leader Networks

Key opinion leader networks (KOLNs) are often created by companies that want to ensure that they have access to thought leaders in the industries in which they operate. While conceptually very similar to innovation networks and leveraging many of the same tactics in their running, KOLNs usually extend beyond the scientific community, and often they have more non-scientists than scientists participating in them.

Often KOLNs have initially been created for regulatory policy or other purposes. The company has identified and enrolled high-profile and influential people in their industry in order to be able to keep track of upcoming areas of concern, gather important insights into the thought processes of decision makers, and create direct pathways to influence those people. KOLNs are also often used to gather reaction to a company's new innovations, new strategies, and changes to existing product and service offerings features. This is a very common strategy in industries like pharmaceuticals and life sciences where the leading research companies all have these networks; we worked in the past with Amgen and Gilead on their KOLNs, and we can say that they have evolved these into a high art form where medical affairs, policy, and regulation can be key to shaping upstream research and development strategies.

Traditional KOLNs are, therefore, often made up of industry participants downstream from the company: go-to-market partners, representatives of major buying groups, service players supporting buyers in other ways, regulators, and those interacting closely with regulators.

One of the industries that have used KOLNs most effectively is the pharmaceutical industry. Here it has long been understood that certain doctors are viewed as thought leaders in their respective areas of specialization. Other doctors look to these KOLs for perspectives on what drugs or devices to use in given situations. When a KOL embraces a new product or solution, it can become very influential with the broader community of doctors focusing in that area.

So too in modern online and social marketing, great effort is being expended to watch who influences whom, and social network analysis is being used to identify the KOLs in any given community. Strategies built to reach, educate, and influence these early adopters to use a new product can prove to be very impactful.

KOLNs can be very valuable from an innovation perspective because these same people who are involved in thought leadership in an industry or geography may also have access to and awareness of new innovations and technologies as they surface. In some regulated industries, the key opinion leaders will, by definition, have exposure to new disruptive innovations that are going through the approval or the regulatory process. The members of the network may also have a better understanding of customer needs and the degree to which an innovation represents enough of an improvement to create a behavior shift away from existing solutions. Finally, having influential individuals in a company's own KOLN may provide valuable insights as to competitive activities since competitors tend to gravitate towards these same people themselves though this raises the issue of exposing your own secrets to others.

In FinTech, to take an example, we have seen an increasing desire from international financial institutions to create KOLNs comprising innovators in their field and in emerging arenas like blockchain, cryptocurrencies, robo-advisors, peer-to-peer lending platforms, crowdfunding, and so on. Because the San Francisco Bay Area has been such an innovation powerhouse in FinTech, with leading "traditional" companies including Bank of America, Schwab, and Wells Fargo, to "new" FinTech players including Apple, Google, Intuit, PayPal, Xoom, and many others, we have seen former and sometimes current employees of these companies being asked to join the KOLNs of international players. While current employees may be limited in what they can offer in the way of insights and guidance, recently departed employees can be great sources of valuable perspectives.

KOLNs are a logical complement to innovation networks,

and they extend the value of the latter by making sure that the customer voice, as well as the other go-to-market voices and regulatory and approval voices are incorporated into the innovation strategy of the corporation.

This tool makes the most sense for industries in which key opinion leaders are essential—it is relatively easy to then extend their mandate to include innovation.

Risk	High
Cost	Low
Implementability	Easier

4. External Advisory Boards

External advisory boards are the next tier of these external innovation networks. External advisory boards are normally made up of people from a variety of areas of activity, not just from the research community. An external advisory board, therefore, is a multi-stakeholder group comprising individuals frequently from business, academia, government, and other areas. The advisory board is used to give perspectives on areas that may be a part of the corporate innovation strategy. They can be valuable as a sounding board for setting priorities, ranking alternatives, and ensuring that the innovation strategy has been made more robust by the perspectives of external advisors who may not have any particular vested interests or internal corporate reasons for supporting particular priorities over others.

External advisory boards are typically formal (whereas KOLNs may be to a large extent informal). This brings advantages and disadvantages. Because an individual is being formally enrolled in an external advisory board, they can be asked to sign confidentiality agreements, non-disclosures, non-competes, etc., in exchange for compensation. Conversely, this formal nature does limit who can participate. Often the most attractive individuals will either not want to limit their own involvements by joining one company's advisory board, or else they may be restricted from doing so by other commitments they may have made.

We have assisted teams to create advisory boards made up of innovators for companies large and small as well as for investing entities. For example, working with Bart and Brad Stephens and Brock Pierce (Brock is also a director of the Bitcoin Foundation) who comprise the general partnership of BlockChain Capital Partners, we built a world-class external advisory board to help the firm shape its perspectives and investment strategies in blockchain technologies. Given Bart, Brad, and Brock's personal experiences and expertise, it was not hard to attract a great advisory board: everyone in financial services worldwide wants to scout and track blockchain, and as one of the most active investors in the space, this team has a great deal of insight.

External advisory boards also have the advantage of some degree of consistency in membership. Advisors are chosen who can have a multi-year role on the board. This provides a sufficient time horizon for it to make sense to invest in educating and training these people into the activities, capabilities, and strategies of the sponsoring company. With that greater understanding comes more targeted and insightful input from the advisory board members.

We think this is a much more powerful tool than its relatively infrequent use would suggest. We recommend a serious look at this for large companies building out their innovation strategies.

Risk	High
Cost	Low
Implementability	Easier

5. Joint Research and Development Agreements

Joint research and development agreements are more formal ways for corporations to collaborate with academic institutions or government agencies. Typically, the joint research and development agreement is a long-term agreement that agrees on specific areas of research and innovation that will be co-funded and co-owned in some degree by both the sponsoring corporation and the innovation institutions, whether they be public or private.

In the early 2000s, we worked with the then Governor of California, Gray Davis, to create the State of California Life Sciences Plan. In parallel with this plan, four Governor Gray Davis Institutes for Science and Innovation were created to advance the frontiers of the new economy. These four institutes were:

- QB3 – The California Institute for Quantitative Biosciences as a joint partnership between UC San Francisco, UC Berkeley, and UC Santa Cruz.
- Calit2 – The California Institute for Telecommunications and Information Technology as a joint partnership between UC San Diego and UC Irvine.
- CNSI – The California Nanosystems Institute as a joint partnership between UC Los Angeles and UC Santa Cruz.
- CITRIS – The Center for Information Technology Research in the Interests of Society as a joint partnership between UC Berkeley, UC Davis, UC Merced, and UC Santa Cruz.

The four joint partnerships were to create focus on areas of promising new innovation surfacing as part of the transition to the Fifth Era. The institutes were tasked with ensuring California continue to be at the leading edge of each innovation domain, and around a billion dollars of public money was earmarked to support their formation and operation.

Of course, no sooner were they created then it became clear that additional funding would be needed, and this would not be forthcoming from public coffers. As a result, the opportunity surfaced for private players to join in the funding of the four institutes in exchange for some influence over setting the innovation focus and access to the innovation output, either through shared ownership or because of privileged access afforded by being a valued sponsor.

In the case of QB3, as an example, the very dynamic executive director Reg Kelly, who had formerly been executive vice chancellor of UC San Francisco, was able to secure support from a wide range of corporate sponsors including Alt, Bayer Healthcare, GE Healthcare, Google/Calico, Johnson & Johnson, Nikon, Roche, and Takeda.

It's particularly important in the creation of joint research and development agreements to ensure that the ownership of innovations is clearly defined. This is frequently the most complex portion of such agreements. Since in many cases the research partner will be wholly or partially government-owned, it can be complex to ensure that a private corporation is able to secure unfettered rights to pursue commercial applications of the new innovations that may surface.

These are long-term commitments and can be capital intensive. We see large companies entering into these types of joint research and development agreements and very often they turn into large-scale construction projects. We wonder whether the capital might have gone further if it had leveraged the entrepreneurial ecosystem rather than funding buildings. Of course, this tool does not need to include a corporate-named building on campus.

Risk	Medium
Cost	Medium
Implementability	Modest

The next three external innovation tools focus on the developer community and technology entrepreneurs with companies in their very first stages of formation. In the case of developer networks and programs, the cost is moderate, and the risk and implementability are not issues although there is a substantial resource cost if the external developer ecosystem becomes large, which is, of course, a beneficial result to aspire to. With corporate and third party incubators, most corporations use these tools as scouting and access devices rather than investment vehicles, which is why we consider them here. Also corporate and third party incubators provide the option of equity investing as well though most corporations waive this for reasons that we will discuss.

6. Developer Networks and Programs

In most areas of technology innovation, there are large populations of external developers who may be working on, or involved with the development of innovations in the specific innovation domains that have been identified as part of the corporate innovation strategy. In order to ensure that those developers prioritize the interests of your company and in order to ensure that they build their own solutions and products leveraging the platforms and standards that are important to your company, it can be very valuable to set up a developer ecosystem and a series of initiatives within it.

All of the most innovative companies have built multi-dimensional developer support portals and organizations. Given their own focus on disruptive innovation and new technologies, this is a requirement for doing business. As a result, each of them operates a friendly ecosystem of developers and derives a great deal of benefit from doing so. In most cases, more "product" is developed by the external ecosystem than by the in-house development teams. As a longtime Apple shareholder, we once sat in on an Apple shareholder meeting in which Steve Jobs was asked why he was not asking Apple developers to improve certain shortcomings in the early apps available on iTunes. Steve's response was that Apple developers would focus only on core foundational software, and he expected that the rest of the world would build the apps that Apple customers would get to see and use. He expected Apple to rely on the world's software engineers, and Apple's job was to support them in the developer network and programs.

These developer networks and programs are all unique to the companies offering them, but most provide a deep and broad online portal and offer free software, development kits, training, access to in-house experts and service personnel, and so on. Sometimes the external developers are so valuable that they will be given the source code to important corporate platforms in exchange for feeding back improvements that they may make as they develop their own solutions on those platforms.

This is a relatively low-risk and easy tool to begin to work with; however, it grows quickly and becomes ever more complex as the external developer community grows and expands. Eventually, it can be a very complex undertaking to be helpful and responsive to a worldwide community of passionate developers who expect real-time, or at least 24-hour responses to complex issues that they may have with your offerings and their own that they have agreed to build on their platforms. The more they need you, the more they demand of you.

Supporting developers is essential for most companies today, so this tool is going to be utilized in some form. The most innovative companies just take it further.

Risk   Medium
Cost   Medium
Implementability Easy

7. Third Party Incubators and Accelerators

Due to the emergence of digital technologies, an increasing number of people have felt able to start entrepreneurial ventures. On the one hand, the costs of doing so have greatly reduced, and on the other hand, the twin forces of globalization and digitalization have expanded addressable markets to the point that start-ups are able to serve customers globally almost from the day they are founded. It has never been easier to launch a new technology-enabled company.

However, with VCs investing later and angel groups selective about the number of formation-phase start-up firms led by first-time founders that they choose to become involved with, there has been a gap in the funding environment for start-ups. First-time founders need some capital, but much more importantly they need a great deal of education, mentorship, and access to capabilities for their start-up. And they need a base location too.

While some angel groups provide such resources, the great demand across the US from first-time founders has led to new models in which some combination of a place to base the company, an environment of support and mentorship, and perhaps a little funding allow for a higher likelihood of moving past the first six months of entrepreneurial-formation activities.

Incubators and accelerators have become this alternative for many first-time CEOs. While somewhat simplified, the distinction between incubators and accelerators is that incubators generally have a non-competitive selection process and focus on formation- to seed-stage companies. Conversely, most accelerators have a highly competitive selection process, are generally centered around an investment business model, last 3 to 6 months, and have intense mentorship programs on-site. There are many alternative models within this new and emerging field; however, some dimensions across which they vary include:

- They may have a physical space, or they may be virtual in nature. Some focus on providing office space only while others focus on the acceleration activities.
- Some charge a monthly or weekly fee for space—perhaps $600 for a desk with access to shared facilities—but do not take equity. This is the "real-estate incubator model" as used at WeWork, founded by Adam Neuman in New York in 2010 that we mentioned earlier in the book, and RocketSpace, founded by Duncan Logan in San Francisco in 2011.
- Others take equity (often in the 5% to 10% range) and may provide a small cash grant (typically between $25,000 and $50,000). This is the "equity-based accelerator model" as practiced by 500 Startups, TechStars, and YCombinator, for example.
- Some may have follow-on funds that can invest in the seed or even Series A rounds of those companies that they see getting the most traction though most start-ups in incubators and accelerators do not move into these phases.
- Additionally, some provide "access to innovation" services for corporate sponsors who want to "scout" the innovation ecosystem and perhaps discover companies for subsequent partnerships.

As a result, the way we see most corporations using third party incubators and accelerators in their external innovation strategies is as scouting devices. Companies agree to sponsor the incubator/accelerator for anything from $50,000 to $150,000 a year typically, and in return, the managers agree to conduct a proactive program to identify start-ups and disruptive technologies that fit the corporate innovation strategy. Both educating the sponsor on what they are seeing, making introductions and often securing first access for the sponsor in potential licensing, go-to market, or acquisition discussions.

For those companies that do not want to only scout one incubator, it can be important to create scouting programs that cover a broader range of such entities including as many as possible of those that include entrepreneurs in the innovation domains of interest. We have helped companies create these cross incubator/ accelerator scouting programs and find them very effective. Given our roles in the angel investor community, we maintain relationships and are active in a number of the leading incubators including Galvanize, Google Launchpad and Accelerator, Microsoft BizSpark, Plug and Play, Rocketspace, Runway, WeWork, and others.

Recently, we have seen a few incubator and accelerator funds begin to appear. While typically backed by large institutional investors, some of these new funds also take investor capital from accredited investors. To date, there are not enough of these funds with years of operation out there for us to be able to make assessments of how they perform and the returns they achieve. The fund general partners argue that the privileged access argument is real, and they typically point to a list of successful graduates that every incubator and accelerator posts on their walls that have gone on to do great things.

For us, the jury is still out on these new funds, but we encourage you to seek them out and make your own determination. For the purpose of this edition, we lump them into the same external innovation tool, but in future years we may need to break them out if they show the ability to capture great returns.

Incubators and accelerators are important parts of the new

external innovation ecosystem and so are an essential component of a corporate external innovation strategy. Some companies go a step further and also create their own – see tool 8 below.

Risk	High
Cost	Low
Implementability	Moderate

8. Corporate Incubators and Accelerators

Once a company has engaged developers throughout their ecosystem, it is almost inevitable that the better developers will begin to take the next step of taking their work and seeing if they can build a company around it. Without question, this does not make sense for most developers and for most of their work, which is better thought of as functionality to be added into other products and platforms. However, there are always diamonds in the rough, and some proportion of the developers have the ambition, capabilities, and experience to turn them into technology entrepreneurs, and their work may have the potential to justify the creation of a fundable company.

If those new companies can be encouraged to build their futures on platforms owned by other companies, there is likely to be substantial value created downstream, at least in the cases of those companies that survive.

With half an eye on the tremendous number of third party incubators and accelerators, some larger companies are choosing to create their own corporate incubators and accelerators to secure this value early, including some of the most innovative and valuable companies in the world. The examples of Microsoft and Google illustrate how this can work.

Microsoft has extended its developer support program into BizSpark, which they describe as a global program that helps start-ups succeed in the following ways:

- BizSpark start-ups receive free access to Microsoft Azure cloud services, software, and support.
- They receive five Visual Studio Enterprise with MSDN subscriptions, each with a $150 monthly Azure credit. This totals $750/month across all five developers to spend on Azure services. These benefits are available for one year.
- On graduation, these companies receive a license grant that provides them software for perpetual use.
- These companies can also gain support and mentorship by Microsoft experts in how to leverage Microsoft platforms into their products and problem-solving support.

Microsoft is rolling out BizSpark globally with three objectives, which they describe as follows:

- Help young and innovative software companies gain valuable experience and expertise in Microsoft technologies, with no upfront costs.
- Help start-ups establish connections with local and global start-up ecosystems: VCs, angels, incubators, accelerators, entrepreneur associations, etc.
- Stimulate vibrant local software ecosystems and promote innovation and interoperability.

A second example is Google Developer Services, which has been extended to include Google Launchpad, Google Launchpad Accelerator, and Google Launchpad Space programs. Roy Glasberg and his team worked hard to create a multi-dimensional program to support entrepreneurs with relevant and ambitious plans around the world. Google Launchpad Accelerator is their capstone program. They describe it as follows:

- Launchpad Accelerator is a program to empower founders by supporting their start-ups through mentorship and equity-free support. The Accelerator leverages all that Google has to offer, to help participating tech start-ups reach their true potential.
- As part of this program, start-ups receive:
  - Equity-free support
  - Two weeks of all-expense-paid training at Google Headquarters in the heart of Silicon Valley
  - Access to Google engineers, resources, and mentors to work closely with Google for 6 months
  - Credits for Google products
  - PR training and global media opportunities
- The program is currently operating in Latin America (Argentina, Brazil, Chile, Colombia, and Mexico), Asia (India, Indonesia, Malaysia, the Philippines, Thailand, and Vietnam), Africa (Kenya, Nigeria, and South Africa), and Europe (Czech Republic, Hungary, and Poland), and there are plans to expand to other countries as well, so stay tuned.

There are many other companies moving down this path, but Microsoft and Google have perhaps the most developed corporate incubator and accelerator programs in the world, and they are viewed as an important component of each company's external innovation strategy.

We do think it is worth considering the use of this tool; however, we recommend most companies begin by scouting other people's incubators and accelerators—let them do the heavy lifting and focus on accessing the entrepreneurs and innovators that they are attracting.

Risk	High
Cost	Low
Implementability	Harder

Next, we consider four external innovations tools that are investment-oriented, enabling companies to become direct and indirect investors in early-stage ventures as well as providing access to scout promising new innovations as they gain traction. These tools begin to bring the risks of early-stage investing into the corporation, which raises substantial issues regarding risk tolerance, ability to accept and support substantial entrepreneurial failure rates, and willingness to create balance sheet vehicles to hold large portfolios of equity positions in. While many have already trod these paths, they do have significant complexities that need to be considered and resolved.

Before we launch into these four tools, we would like to provide some context around the realities of early-stage investment in the US. Sidebar 4 is an abstract from a white paper that we co-authored in 2016 where we sought to demystify the realities of who backs start-ups in the US. It turns out that contrary to conventional wisdom, perhaps 80% or so of the equity provided to start-ups in their seed and formation rounds in the US comes from angel investors with VCs providing some 15% and other types of investors providing the remaining 5% of the capital.

Sidebar 7: Do VCs Back Start-ups?

The traditional model of start-up funding has always held that investors in technology companies at inception include the entrepreneurs themselves, their friends and families, and angel investors, who are willing to invest their own money into the new companies. Later, early- and late-stage VC funds may become investors in these start-ups, but they only do so once the company has matured to a point that it is considered investable by the VC (see Exhibit 24). However, in the main, people simplify this multi-part funding cycle into a simple premise—VCs back start-ups.

Exhibit 24

Equity Capital for Technology Entrepreneurs

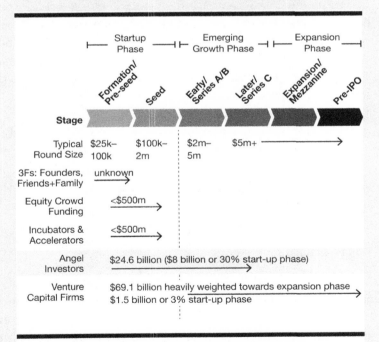

Sources: Jeffrey E. Sohl, Robert Wiltbank, Ian Hathaway, Crowdnetic, ACA, NVCA, Pricewaterhouse Coopers, Dow Jones Venture Source, Fifth Era, LLC

But, this has been changing very rapidly, and, as a result, the conventional wisdom is now misleading.

According to the most recent NVCA 2017 Yearbook, VCs have effectively stopped seeding most start-ups in the US:

For the full year 2016, US VCs invested $69 billion but only into 7,750 companies.

Of this $69 billion, the majority went to mid-stage and pre-IPO companies and not start-ups. Only approximately $1.5 billion or 3% of the venture capital funding was in the seed or earlier rounds when companies were in their initial start-up phase. Venture capitalists backed fewer seed and earlier companies in 2015 than in any year since 1995.

In short, today US VCs are focusing their efforts and capital on emerging-growth companies and very few start-ups receive any funding from VCs until they can justify valuations in the double digit millions of dollars – typically a series A round early stage investment. VCs simply do not deploy material capital into the start-up phase of a company's lifecycle in the US (formation- and seed-stage funding). Instead, US technology companies seeking VC capital will need to have moved a long way beyond a business strategy—they will have established their company, formed their founding team, built their initial products, perhaps begun to serve customers in the marketplace, and might even be generating substantial revenue—before a VC will consider them for an investment. VCs back very few start-ups.

What Changed?

After the 2008 crisis, US VCs were confronted by a substantial shake-out and a flight of capital to leading firms. The best VCs got much larger while others, in the face of this flight of capital, ceased to invest and instead focused on their existing portfolios. Many VCs went out of business altogether. As the NVCA 2016 Yearbook points out:

The number of VC firms in the US is today only 898, down from 1,009 in 2005.

Interestingly, while the number of firms has declined, the money managed has increased. The average firm now manages $243.6 million, and the largest fund raised was a whopping $4.3 billion.

In 2015 alone, the VCs raised an additional $41.6 billion, which they needed to invest.

This trend of fewer funds and fewer professionals managing ever-larger sums of money gives rise to some simple consequences:

VCs prefer to put larger amounts of money into each deal that they back.

In addition, while the larger VC firms are backing more companies, they are doing so in later stages. Instead of investing in start-ups at the formation and seed stages, they are investing in those companies later in their lifecycles.

Many VCs are putting the bulk of their money to work in well-established later-stage growth firms or as pre-IPO capital, essentially what used to be known as expansion capital investing.

Furthermore, many VCs are also participating in "non-venture-related investments," including investing in debt, buyouts, recapitalizations, secondary purchases, IPOs, and public companies, such as PIPES (private investments in public entities), investments which the proceeds are primarily intended for acquisition, such as roll-ups, change of ownership, and other forms of private equity that are not even captured in the statistics of the NVCA.

In short, and with a few exceptions, VCs have become expansion capital investors, rather than start-up investors. And this is unlikely to change given the massive amount of capital that is today managed by US VCs. If not VCs, then who does back start-ups?

By the relative numbers, it can be seen that angel investors are much more important for most companies in their start-up phase of life compared to VCs who, for the most part, only invest in angel-backed companies once they have significant traction that justifies larger investment rounds (see Exhibit 25). The angels of the US are seeding most US technology start-ups.

Exhibit 25

Angels Back Most US Start-ups

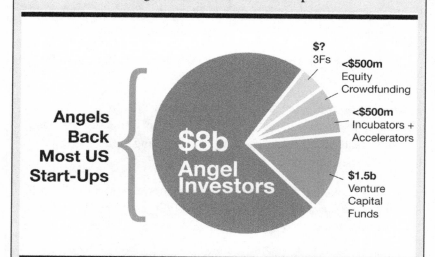

* Formation and seed rounds – estimates from sources
Sources: Jeffrey E. Sohl, Robert Wiltbank, Ian Hathaway, Crowdnetic, ACA, NVCA, Pricewaterhouse Coopers, Dow Jones Venture Source, Fifth Era, LLC

With this as context, let us now review the four external innovation tools focused on early-stage investing in order to gain access to new innovations early in their life cycles.

9. Crowdfunding Investments

Over the last few years, the US has worked towards making it easier for the broader population to invest in small businesses in order to democratize start-up investing beyond organized VC funds and accredited angel investors. This has seen the passing of the Jumpstart Our Business Start-ups Act or JOBS Act. First signed into law by President Obama in 2012, the act continues to be made into law as the SEC reviews and releases additional components of regulation. The JOBS Act as originally passed would, among other things, do the following:

- Allow for an increase in the number of shareholders a company may have before being required to register its common stock with the SEC and become a publicly reporting company.
- Provide an exemption from the need to register public offerings with the SEC that would allow the use of Internet funding portals, including "equity crowdfunding platforms" (with certain limits on how much an investor can invest through these portals).
- Create a new definition of "emerging-growth companies" as those with less than $1 billion in revenues.
- Relieve these companies from some regulatory and disclosure requirements when they go public.
- Lift the ban on "general solicitation" and advertising of specific kinds of private placements.

The JOBS Act has stimulated the formation of a very large number of "equity crowdfunding" platforms and businesses. While the potential may be significant in terms of providing additional avenues for start-ups to receive funding, the current progress is modest. Crowdnetic, which tracks the major crowdfunding platforms in the US, reports that from September 23, 2013, through September 23, 2015 (two years):

- There were 6,063 distinct offerings, of which 1,596 were successful in raising commitments of $870 million for an average of $545,122 per successful issuer.
- California alone accounted for 472 of the successful offerings raising $270 million.
- The top three sectors benefitting were real-estate development, real-estate investment, and oil and gas production and pipelines—thus, technology start-ups were not the leading recipients of equity crowdfunding in that time period.
- The two real-estate sectors accounted for $208.3 million of the $870 million (23.9%) in total commitments made through equity crowdfunding platforms tracked by Crowdnetic.

So, while crowdfunding shows promise in terms of being a viable approach to backing start-ups, in practice the $870 million raised to date has seen a majority invested outside technology start-ups. Furthermore, that $870 million pales in comparison to the more than $69 billion the VCs invest primarily in later-stage rounds and the $24.6 billion that the angels invest primarily in formation through Series A rounds.

However, crowdfunding might be a good way for you to dip a toe into being an investor in early-stage technology companies. The advantages are that you can make very small investments, don't need to do your own extensive due diligence, and can, as a result, build a large diversified portfolio quickly. Perhaps the leading equity crowdfunding platform in the US is AngelList founded by Nadal Ravikant in 2010. Today AngelList is backed by a number of venture investors, including CSC Group of China, which makes additional capital available to deals that have been taken through the crowdfunding process. Among the syndicate managers who are most active on AngelList is Gil Penchina, one of the early executives at eBay and a prolific investor.

We are also seeing a few very creative uses of crowdfunding among the most innovative companies. In this regard, Amazon stands out with the use of a crowdsourcing platform that enables aspiring screenwriters to propose original titles for Amazon-funded shows that can be released on Amazon's own platforms, on other digital platforms, or even in broader releases across physical distribution too. Amazon has done something similar in video games, sponsoring original titles for its own streaming video game network, Twitch, as well as for other means of distribution. This "captive" crowdsourcing in which the corporation provides the capital for the best innovations is certainly worth keeping an eye on.

The disadvantages are that crowdfunding is new and we do not yet know the returns or failure rates for the types of deals appearing on the platforms. It will likely be another 5 or 10 years before that becomes clear. Additionally, you don't know exactly what due diligence has been done and by whom. In some cases the syndicate managers who are putting forward investment opportunities may not have your interests at heart: they get compensated by sharing any returns you make, so in some cases, they may care more about getting you to invest than about the risk-adjusted return that you will experience. So, as with all investing, you need to do your own due diligence, uncover other people's motivations and vested interests, and only invest when you are sure you know the lay of the land.

Some companies are finding scouting crowdfunding beneficial, but we have yet to see very active corporate investors on crowdfunding platforms.

Risk	High
Cost	Low
Implementability	Moderate

10. Angel Co-Investment Funds

Back in 1997, we had begun to make a few angel investments in the run-up to the dotcom boom and bust. At the time we were both full-time consulting partners at AT Kearney, but entrepreneurs were beginning to approach us for funding and we had capital to invest. As the years went by, we saw our small portfolio beginning to include some winners, and so in 2000 after leaving Gap we explored full-time angel investing but quickly found you can't be an angel by yourself. This is a team game. You need access to a broader funnel of opportunities, you need to do due diligence and negotiate your terms and conditions in a group, and it takes a whole band of angels to bring all the ongoing support an early-stage company needs to begin to get traction.

As a result, we and many angels have begun to focus on approaches that allow for the building of large portfolios of angel-backed companies to create diversification with the expectation that in larger numbers of companies exist the prospect of both capturing more innovation in the net and better returns. This includes allowing participation of non-angel investors.

This is a relatively new option. Some angel groups have created co-investment vehicles that invest in all or some of the companies that their angel groups back. At Band of Angels where we have been members for a decade, Ian Sobieski, who is the president, is also general partner of the Acorn Fund, which selectively backs companies that his angel members are investing in. So too at Angels' Forum where the founder, Carol Sands, is also the lead partner in the Halo Funds. At Keiretsu Forum, we have created a whole family of such funds within Keiretsu Capital, including three funds that invest in the same rounds as the angels and a real-estate fund to give members access to a diversified real-estate fund portfolio.

Most of these angel co-investment funds are intended to solve the diversification challenge for the active angel members of the group, as well as help them invest in areas they may be uncomfortable directly investing in or in deals that they may have otherwise missed. At Keiretsu Capital, our funds each invest in more than 40 companies so that if our angels have backed perhaps 10 or 15 companies directly, they can supplement their portfolio with another 40 through each fund they invest in.

A handful of these angel co-investment funds may be open to investors, who are not members of the angel group and who are not active angel investors. This provides a powerful opportunity to people who would otherwise not have access to disruptive technology companies being backed by the leading angel investors. In our funds, we have investors from Europe and Asia who are investing specifically because they want some of their capital to go into US technology companies in the early stage of funding, but they would not otherwise be able to make investments in these companies.

Since Keiretsu Forum is the most active venture investor by number of deals in the US (more than 160 companies backed in 2016), the network provides a powerful deal-flow funnel for the co-investment funds to use to create portfolios of diversified Fifth Era emerging technology companies. Even more so, Keiretsu, because of its position as the largest angel group, also sees great deals syndicated to it from other leading angel groups (and vice versa). So, even more opportunities enter the funnel each cycle.

Angel co-investment funds allow passive investors (or active) to put capital to work across large portfolios of Fifth Era companies that other active angel investors have backed with their own capital. This is the purest economic signal since you are committing capital only after experienced angel investors have completed all of their due diligence, made the decision to invest their own capital, and the round is close to closing.

The major disadvantages are similar to the venture capital fund disadvantages. Funds charge fees and your returns are reduced as a result. If you could have been a direct and active angel investor, investing your capital without fees directly into the companies a large number of times, then you would have a higher return at the end of the day than by investing through an angel co-investment fund.

For a corporation creating an external innovation strategy, this is a new and novel approach to scout a large number of companies and secure early stage access without needing to put substantial capital to work.

Risk	Medium
Cost	Medium
Implementability	Moderate

11. Venture Capital Funds

The next tool is to utilize venture capitalists and their funds both to invest directly into companies and also as a scouting tool.

Direct investment into Fifth Era companies in their earliest stages when the returns are likely to be the largest seems to be a good option, based upon the words we have written to this point. The expected returns are high—perhaps the highest of any current asset class in America. The risk is substantial, at 50% to 70% failure on average, but there is plenty of evidence that 10% of the investments will return 5 times or more, and in so doing, that handful will drive your average return in the mid- to high-20% annual returns. There is real risk that if you don't invest enough times, you may expose yourself to the risk of total capital loss, but if you invest in 48 or more companies, you seem to have around 95% likelihood of earning the asset class return while even at 24 investments you are at a 90% probability level.

Back in the 1980s and 1990s, the venture capitalist options really were the best way to back start-ups. But over the last few years, they have become more focused on the rounds of capital following the early stage. Today, venture capitalists put most of their capital to work in the mid- and late stages of venture capital funding. This means that the venture capital funds tool is most valuable for accessing later stage companies and has become less powerful for tapping into early stage innovations.

Today we do see companies investing through venture capital funds in order to gain access to interesting technologies and companies. However, this tends to be a tool to utilize in countries where you don't have direct access. In addition, the rise of venture exchanges of all sorts has presented alternative ways to scout the VC-backed companies without the need to be an investor in their funds (tool 13).

In most countries where corporations have a strong presence, they lean towards creating their own corporate venture funds as described in tool 12 below.

Risk	Medium
Cost	Medium
Implementability	Moderate

12. Corporate Venture Funds

Unlike the relatively recent phenomenon in which corporations have looked at third party incubators and accelerators, and created their own corporate versions, corporate venture funds are a very long-standing and established tool for a company to tap into external innovations.

The National Venture Capital Association has a specific track for corporate venture groups and tracks them with the help of PricewaterhouseCoopers and Thomson Reuters. They estimated that corporate venture groups deployed over $1.2 billion in 198 deals in the entrepreneurial ecosystem in the second quarter of 2016. Indeed, around 20% of all deals backed by venture capital firms included some participation by corporate venture groups. This percentage holds broadly true across innovation domains with both software and biotechnology sectors receiving in the order of 20% of their capital this way.

There are a great many ways to create a corporate venture group, and there are very complex issues that arise as you do so. We have talked with and/or assisted leading companies as they considered the formation of such groups including companies as diverse as Agilent, Alphabet/Google (Google Ventures and Google Capital), Axel Springer, Bank of America, BT, EDS, HP, IBM, Intel, Microsoft, and the consulting firms AT Kearney and Monitor Group, to name a few. Significant issues that arise include:

- What will be the ongoing focus of the group, and what will it not focus on?
- What capital will it be able to invest, and what will be the investment thesis by geography, sector, stage, and size of investment?
- What will be the requirements for an investment including all terms and conditions, and what will be the positive and negative implications of these requirements?
- Who will compose the decision-making team?
- How will they be compensated? Salaries, bonuses, carry points?
- Given the long timeframes associated with investing in technology companies, what incentives will both align

and protect the investment professionals?

- How will investment professionals' objectives be aligned with those of the senior leadership team at the outset and over time?
- How will "adverse" behaviors be avoided given the above?
- What will the company do with "orphan" investments as strategies change over time?

At Google Ventures (now GV) more than 300 companies have been invested in since GV's formation in 2009. These companies focus on innovation domains that Alphabet/Google prioritized in its innovation strategy, including life sciences, healthcare, artificial intelligence, robotics, transportation, cybersecurity, and agriculture. In addition to providing capital, GV is tasked with helping the portfolio companies interface with Google so as to be able to access all of the technologies, people, and resources of the company worldwide.

On balance we have found that while corporate venture groups can be very powerful in furthering the strategic aims of their host corporations, a significant period of discussion, alignment, and agreements needs to be held before greenlighting a new group, and this dialogue needs to continue on a regular basis to ensure that the corporate venture group is kept focused and relevant to the corporate priorities and that interests do not diverge with time. When this dialogue is not ongoing, we have seen significant challenges surface, which can become quite difficult to resolve.

Risk	Medium
Cost	Medium
Implementability	Harder

Finally, we review five external innovation tools focused on providing access to promising companies and their innovations enabling licensing agreements, go-to-market partnerships, joint ventures, and acquisitions. In most cases, these will be used to enable corporate involvement with later-stage and pre-IPO companies, including "unicorns," and newly minted public companies. The risk will in most cases have fallen because these companies have proven demand for their products and services although in many cases they may not have proven a profitable business model. Costs will be skyrocketing as valuations become very high for disruptive innovation companies with high growth expectations. These deals (and they are almost always a deal of some sort) will be complex to implement as multiple stakeholders will need to be engaged, and oftentimes there will be a number of competitors wanting to play in opposition to your company, creating "seller markets" in competitive bidding and auction processes.

13. Venture Exchanges

Once a company has considered creating its own corporate venture team or being formally allied with a venture capitalist or an investor in venture capital funds, then it may make sense to hold regular venture exchanges. A venture exchange is a structured environment in which a select group of venture funds are invited to bring portfolio companies that meet the priorities and interests of the corporation's innovation strategy. By entering into a formal long-term relationship with a handful of venture capitalists, corporations can then open up their innovation strategy to those venture capitalists and encourage them to bring companies that meet the criteria and the priorities of the corporation's strategy.

During 2007 to 2009 we formed and operated a venture exchange with our then partner Colin Wiel for the angel group Keiretsu Forum. Our intent was to expose the very large portfolio of companies that Keiretsu angels had backed to a select group of top-tier Silicon Valley venture capital firms and a smaller group of corporate venture teams. On a quarterly basis, we would bring chosen companies to meet with the investment professionals of each venture group and have the CEOs present their companies, strategies, and ways that they would benefit from additional rounds of capital and the capabilities and assets that a large company might bring to bear. We found that every meeting was interesting and valuable, but that very few investment rounds came out of these meetings. In retrospect, this should not be a surprise since as we have shown, venture capital firms only invest in a handful of companies each year with the average firm only making perhaps 2 to 4 investments per year. Thus, the chances that a venture exchange introduction would lead to an investment are small.

Conversely, for a corporate innovation effort venture exchanges can be much more valuable, primarily as educational and relationship-building exercises and because deals in which companies bring their expertise to bear are far more numerous than ones in which they end up being investors. Tools 14 to 17 detail just why this is the case and describe the range of actions a corporate team may be able to consider as they meet companies in a venture exchange setting.

Today there has been a proliferation of these exchanges, from small group settings in which a top-tier venture capital firm brings a selected company or two to meet a handful of companies one-on-one as part of a roadshow, to massive conferences, like TechCrunch Disrupt, SXSW, or WebSummit, in which hundreds of CEOs of small companies pitch to crowds of scores or even hundreds of investment professionals. Their popularity demonstrates that both presenters and attendees must believe they are getting value from these exchanges of information, but we don't see too many investment rounds occurring at or after them.

We think the great value of this tool is the learning that can be derived by participating and seeing the portfolio companies and by hearing what they have developed and are bringing to market.

With this scouting and learning goal in mind, we highly recommend venture exchanges of all sorts be built into an overall external innovation strategy. But don't look to make too many investments in them.

Risk	Low
Cost	High
Implementability	Easier

14. In-Licensing Programs

Viewed from the perspective of emerging technology companies, the most likely way for them to get to a successful exit is for them to sell their company at some point to a larger company that will then exploit the technologies and take them to market. It's possible for a small company to accelerate their go-to-market strategy and begin to form relationships with potential acquirers by licensing out their technologies and products either in geographies, industries, or domains that they are unlikely to serve themselves directly. From the point of view of the emerging company, this is a practical strategy for exploiting its innovations more rapidly than would be the case if it waited until it had scale and scope to do it with its own resources.

From the point of view of a large company, a structured in-licensing program can be a very effective way of gathering disruptive innovations in-house and taking them to market in areas where the emerging company cannot play. This works well as a long-term strategy for ensuring a seat at the table if and when the company is up for sale, as most will eventually be.

This has been a tool exploited throughout the pharmaceutical and life sciences industry, and a lot can be learned by observing how the most active larger companies lock in specific drugs and sometimes entire companies through an aggressive in-licensing program. Famously European pharmaceutical companies have used this tool as a lever into discussions with US biotechnology companies. Roche used this strategy to lock in first-position advantage with Genentech, Novartis began its discussion that led to the acquisition of Chiron in this way, as so too did Sanofi with Genzyme.

In-licensing programs require that the licensor company be very clear on the products and services that it wants to take to market and also require a comprehensive scouting of potential solutions and a prioritization of which ones make sense to license.

In-licensing programs can also be accompanied by patent programs where large companies establish or buy large numbers of patents that can make it difficult for small companies to bring their products to market in an unimpeded way, or conversely they can provide leverage to encourage those small companies to collaborate in bringing products to market together.

Finally, it can be very productive to combine an "in-licensing program" with a simultaneous "out-licensing" program. Since most large companies have orphan technologies and innovations that they are not using, and comprehensive external innovation strategies tend to exacerbate this reality, an out-licensing strategy can be very productive. This can be helpful both to monetize innovations that would otherwise go unutilized and sometimes to trade innovations with others who may value what you have much more highly than you and who may be willing to give you what you want in exchange.

Risk	Medium
Cost	Medium
Implementability	Moderate

15. Go-to-Market Partnerships

If there is one thing that makes or breaks a new disruptive innovation company, it is securing its first customers and making sure the new innovation meets their needs. As the Harvard professor and author Clayton Christensen famously remarked, "As a general rule, if you have a product that doesn't get the job done that a customer is needing to get done, then often you have to offer it for zero. Because if you ask for money for it—because if it doesn't do the job well, they won't pay for it." But the entrepreneurial dilemma is that most new companies don't have any customers to try their product, and they don't have the scale and scope to support those first customers as they try and figure out how to use the product when it is still not "quite good enough."

New disruptive innovations often never get a chance to cross the chasm because they can't get a few good customers to try them. Big companies can help small ones solve this dilemma.

Big companies can solve this first because they can be customers themselves. They can try a product, support it with their own resources, give feedback, and make it better—all in-house. And they quickly can be powerful reference cases. For a small company, having a big company say it uses the product, has made sure it works well, and recommends it to others can be the most powerful early driver of success possible.

Because big companies have lots of customers of their own, they can bring a product to market much more powerfully if they want to. However, they need to be careful of course because their own reputation with customers will be at stake.

Apple and Google do this very well in their support of new innovations in each of the Apple and Google app stores respectively. Both companies have large teams of people in developer services that are always helping small app developers improve their products. In Google Accelerator, as an example, Roy

Glasberg, Josh Yellin, and the team give promising new companies access to whatever Google people and resources can be found to help optimize the new innovative offerings. Then those "optimized" products are brought to market in the app store (if they are apps) or through other Google sales channels if appropriate. While there may be many reasons for helping companies in this way (revenue, insight, customer satisfaction, local government support, and so on) the bottom line is that Google can help small companies succeed overnight. The stamp of approval that comes from Google saying it believes in this product opens doors around the world. That stamp of approval may say "certified developer," "editor's choice," or something else that denotes a product that Google believes is good for customers. Such a stamp of approval cuts through the clutter much better than anything the innovator can say about themselves.

The go-to-market tool is all about looking at your own innovation strategy, determining what innovations you need to bring to market on behalf of your own customers, seeing what you have in your own internal pipeline, filling the gaps by identifying new innovations that are in the hands of smaller external players that don't have the resources to properly bring them to market, and then reaching out and creating a partnership of mutual benefit in which you fill their gap and they fill yours.

This strategy can work in-market and in-industry, which is to say you can bring a product to market in the country where both you and the external innovator are active and in the industry where you are both focusing. But that tends to raise issues because the innovator, if capitalized, will have their own aspirations to bring their own innovations to market in this particular case. Therefore, in-market in-industry go-to-market partnerships tend to be most prevalent where the innovator does not have any aspiration to become a company; they tend to be partnerships with scientists, research institutions, and so forth, similar to the partnerships we described with regard to the California Institutes created by Governor Gray Davis.

Conversely, out-of-market out-of-industry go-to-market partnerships tend to be obvious to the smaller innovator. They have no aspirations, capabilities, or short-term resources to serve customers in other countries across the globe in industries that they don't understand. These tend to be easy deals to do, but the burden of figuring out how to make the innovation work and how to support it falls completely on the shoulders of the larger company, which creates work, cost, and risk.

We favor the two middle roads that are out-of-market/in-industry and in-market/out-of-industry. Specifically, we favor the former.

In the out-of-market/in-industry partnership the larger company is based in some other region or country but in the same industry that the innovator has been building their new product. The larger company then approaches the smaller and offers to accelerate go-to-market activities in this other part of the world, in turn bringing in much-needed revenue earlier than would otherwise occur for the smaller company.

This is the favorite strategy of many Chinese, Japanese, and Korean companies that we see active in Silicon Valley. They are scouting the new innovations of the US clusters of innovation, negotiating country or broad Asian/ASEAN go-to-market partnerships, and then working to implement the innovation in their region.

In VR/AR, as just one example, we see companies like HTC, Lenovo, Samsung, Tencent, and ZTE being very aggressive in licensing Asian rights to new US technologies. HTC/Vive and Samsung have created entire incubator programs specifically to secure these rights on promising teams and technologies, and have large Silicon Valley presences working on this strategy. One of the companies we have backed Waygate/VRTV and the team of

Ben Cooley, Carlo Morgantini, and Andre Blanadet were courted in just this way and signed an initial period of collaboration with HTC.

We worked with Chinese and Japanese companies for more than a decade building these Silicon Valley and US go-to-market presences, including with Ningbo Shanshan Group, Hitachi, Kingsoft, Talkweb, and Tencent. Our partner James Zhang at Concept Art House is an expert in building these cross-Pacific partnerships for bringing US and European digital entertainment to China and Chinese blockbuster games to the Western markets, and sees this as a critical need on both sides of the Pacific specifically because without a local market player, all of the minutia of localizing and fitting an overseas product to local customer needs just won't be done right. In digital entertainment, like video games, VR, film, and so on, these subtle adjustments may make all the difference between success and outright failure.

The out-of-market/in-industry partnership is a tool that every external innovation strategy must include.

Risk	Low to Medium
Cost	Medium to High
Implementability	Easy to Moderate

16. Joint Venture Programs

Where the innovator and their company, if they have one, is small and relatively weak you don't need a joint venture with them. You just use tools 14 or 15 to secure access to their innovation, in-licensing, and go-to-market partnerships respectively.

But if the innovator is not weak, if they are a venture capital-backed unicorn with billions of dollars of market value and hundreds of millions of dollars in the bank, what then?

Here there needs to be a more compelling story than just

"You can't get to this now, so we will help you accelerate." In this particular situation, there need to be very good reasons why the unicorn needs to release a part of its global opportunity to a partner corporation.

A lot of theory has been written on joint ventures, and each of our alma maters, McKinsey, AT Kearney, Monitor Group, and Booz, have groups of practitioners that focus on creating large multi-national joint ventures with all of the complex issues associated with them.

We tended to focus more on joint ventures between private innovative Silicon Valley companies and public and private international players that want to bring their US innovations to overseas markets. Even still, we find much of the findings of our former partners still relevant in these cases too.

For the purpose of this book, we will simply say that if you really need to work with a holder of a new disruptive innovation that is central to your innovation strategy but which you can't secure in a simpler way, then maybe a joint venture can be the correct answer; however, the design phase will be long and complex, and needs to be so because joint ventures are also very complex to make work.

Unfortunately, we have seen most joint ventures become problematic as the respective interests of the two parties diverge over time. We believe that this is a common finding. Joint ventures can be powerful tools in the external innovation toolkit, but they are hard to design, hard to make successful, and tend to have relatively short lives during which the partners remain aligned, after which the process of separation can be a complex and difficult one to execute together.

Risk	Low to Medium
Cost	High to Medium
Implementability	Hard

17. Acquisition Programs

As noted above, the majority of small companies will eventually exit by selling themselves to larger companies. For large companies, this raises the opportunity to have structured programs of dialogue with small companies as they develop and get themselves to a place that makes sense to bring them into the consideration set for an acquisition.

Large companies can, therefore, create radar screens in which they scout and track promising candidates, engage them in conversations early, and position their companies as the best possible acquirer if an acquisition eventually seems to make sense. Working with corporate development teams, the innovation teams can operate a broad scouting, scanning, tracking, and interaction program to ensure that good acquisition opportunities are constantly surfaced and considered.

Most of the other tools we have described fuel an acquisition program of this type.

As examples, innovation networks allow the corporate development team to see what new research and development breakthroughs are coming onto the horizon; third party incubators let them know what entrepreneurs are getting ready to bring to market; angel co-investment and venture capital-funded LP positions ensure that they have a small stake in a large number of potential acquisitions; and go-to-market partnerships make you a preferred acquirer and make it harder for a competitor to displace you. These and many of the other external innovation tools have their respective roles in a well-structured corporate acquisition program aimed at bringing in internal innovations to the company.

The issues with a corporate acquisition program are mostly around why and when to move, with whom, and how to make sure things go well after you are together. Crucial questions to consider around an acquisition include the following:

- What innovations on the corporate innovation strategy will not be met with internal and external efforts already in place?
- Should these gaps in the strategy be filled early with small acquisitions that still have a substantial risk but which can be bought cheaply?
- Or conversely, should the corporation wait until the likelihood of failure of the innovation has diminished as it gets proved in the marketplace, knowing the cost of the acquisition will greatly increase as the potential acquisition crosses the chasm and sees its market capitalization accelerate?
- Of all the potential acquisitions, which look most promising, which look most likely to want to exit, and which are you well positioned to win?
- How will you begin the dialogue: early but risk pushing up the value? Later but risk reading an announcement that someone else already did the deal?
- Since most acquisitions fail, how will you make sure you are a good new owner of innovation-based acquisitions? Since so much of value may be in the heads of the handful of people you are buying, how will you keep them onboard and motivated when they work for you?

After decades working with buyers and sellers of innovation-based companies and representing them on both sides of the table, we don't think there is a right or wrong answer to any of these questions. It all depends, and the answers need to be bespoke tailored to the cloth. When one of the companies we had backed, Soundwave, was in negotiations to be acquired by Spotify, we were able to see firsthand just how clearly Spotify had thought through how to leverage the innovations that Soundwave had created as well as the best ways to make sure that the Soundwave team of innovators felt excited about joining and remaining with Spotify for the future. Sitting on the other side of the table as directors at technology-based companies like First Data, Fiserv, Unisys, and Xoom, we have seen the other side of that coin and been involved in long and deep discussions about how to make acquisitions work without losing either the breakthroughs that drive the value capture or the innovators that will be needed to execute the strategy post-acquisition.

Historically, many large corporations preferred to wait until the risk of failure was diminished. Their boards were filled with people who needed to see supporting discounted cash flow projections that could support the acquisition prices, and they were fearful of buying a "clunker" on their watch whereby a new innovation-based acquisition just did not deliver the goods that comprised the acquisition rationale. Cisco was famous for making mid-sized to larger acquisitions, but only once the innovations were proven in the market; for them the increased cost they would pay was worth the reduction in risk that market proof points afforded. They saw so much economic upside by scaling up the innovation across their own footprint that they were willing to pay the increased exit price.

An outstanding example of a market-leading company that was created through many acquisitions of innovative companies is Fiserv, the leading American financial services technology provider. Fiserv has made more than 150 acquisitions over the last 25 years including more recent large acquisitions of M-Com (mobile banking applications), CashEdge//Popmoney (electronic funds transfer), Open Solutions (DNA), and Guardian Analytics (security products for online banking channels). This strategy has proven very successful in consistently driving Fiserv shareholder value creation as well as keeping it at the forefront of innovation in its industry.

Today all of the most innovative companies are making large billion-dollar and up acquisitions. Examples include Alphabet/ Google buying DoubleClick, YouTube, and Nest; Apple buying Beats; Facebook buying Instagram, Oculus, and WhatsApp; Microsoft buying LinkedIn, Mojang, Nokia, Skype, and Yammer; and Tesla buying SolarCity.

While Jeff Bezos has balked at paying more than $1 billion in an acquisition, his large acquisitions of Twitch, Zappos, and Kiva almost make the over-a-billion-dollar list.

In addition to these billion-dollar-plus acquisitions, every one of the most innovative companies has a much more active program of many small acquisitions underway. These range from acquisitions of viable companies with products that are doing well and fit well into the innovation strategy, to teams with unfinished or even failing products but valuable capabilities. Right down at the smallest end of the spectrum are "acquihires," in which a company buys a small company really only for the team of innovators and frequently with the intent of closing down the acquisition on closing.

To make the point crystal clear, here is the list of acquisitions made by Facebook in just the last five years (thank you Wikipedia and Crunchbase for helping us compile this list):

2011
- Rel8tion – mobile advertising, WA, US
- Beluga – group messaging, CA, US
- Snaptu – mobile app developer, London, UK
- RecRec – computer vision, CA, US
- DayTum – information graphics, NY, US
- Sofa – software design, Amsterdam, Netherlands
- MailRank – email prioritization, NY, US
- Push Pop Press – digital publishing, CA, US

- Friend.ly – social casual Q&A service app, CA, US
- Strobe – HTML5 mobile apps, SproutCore, CA, US
- Gowalla – location-based services, TX, US

2012

- Caffeinated Mind – in-browser file transfer, CA, US
- Instagram – photo-sharing, CA, US
- Tagtile – customer loyalty app, CA, US
- Glancee – social discovery platform, CA, US
- Lightbox.com – photo-sharing, London, UK
- Karma – social gifting, CA, US
- Face.com – face recognition platform, Tel Aviv, Israel
- Spool – mobile bookmarking and sharing content, CA, US
- Acrylic software – RSS app Pulp and secure database app wallet, Vancouver, Canada
- Threadsy – social aggregator, CA, US

2013

- Atlas Solutions – advertising suite, WA, US
- Osmeta – mobile software, CA, US
- Hot studio - design agency, NY, US
- Spaceport – cross platform game framework, CA, US
- Parse – mobile app backends, CA, US
- Monoidics – automatic verification software, London, UK
- Jibbigo – speech translation, PA, US
- Onavo – mobile analytics, Tel Aviv, Israel
- Sport Stream – sports conversation analysis, CA, US

2014

- Little Eye Labs – performance analysis and monitoring, Bengaluru, India
- Branch – web conversation platform, NY, US
- WhatsApp – mobile instant messaging, CA, US
- Oculus VR – VR technology, CA, US
- Ascenta – high altitude UAVs, Somerset, UK

- Proto Geooy – fitness tracking app, Helsinki, Finland
- Pryte – single click buying of data, Helsinki, Finland
- PrivateCore – secure server technology, CA, US
- LiveRail – publisher monetization platform, CA, US
- Wave Group Sound – sound studio, CA, US

2015

- Wit.ai – speech recognition, CA, US
- Quickfire Networks – video compression, CA, US
- TheFind Inc - eCommerce, CA, US
- Teehan+Lax – digital experience agency, Toronto, Canada
- Surreal Vision – computer vision and augmented reality, London, UK
- Pebbies – computer vision and augmented reality, Kfar Saba, Israel

2016

- MSQRD – visual effects, Minsk, Belarus
- Two Big Ears – spatial audio, Scotland, UK
- Nascent Objects – cloud connected products, CA, US
- Eyegroove – music social network, CA, US
- Endaga – rural mobile networks, CA, US
- Crowdtangle – social tracking, MD, US
- Infiniled – Oculus VR, Cork, Ireland
- Faciometrics – computer vision and machine learning, PA, US

Now we take several important lessons away from this list:

- Facebook, one of the world's most innovative companies, is buying a larger number of other innovative companies and teams every year.
- If you compare the acquisitions with the list of strategically important innovation domains that Face-

book described as its focus in Chapter 6 (i.e., the top leadership team knows and communicates innovation strategy), you will see the driving force behind most of these acquisitions:

- Connectivity – including terrestrial solutions, telco infrastructure, free basics, satellites, drones, and lasers
- Artificial Intelligence – including vision, language, reasoning, and planning
- VR/AR – including social VR, mobile VR, Oculus Rift, touch, and AR technologies

- It is remarkable how many of the acquired companies are Silicon Valley or California companies; yes, Facebook itself is based there, but we think it reflects the remarkable innovation-based economy of California and the implication for the critical need to scout it if you are going to play this external innovation game.
- Most other acquisitions come from a small number of other innovations clusters primarily in Seattle, New York, and London.

Mark Zuckerberg was interviewed in January 2017 about his company's innovation acquisition program by *Business Insider.* He shared four key acquisition program guiding principles:

- Build relationships first.
- Have a shared vision.
- Sometimes use scare tactics ("You can't do this by yourself").
- Move fast and buy things.

Business Insider goes on to quote Zuckerberg as saying, "So being able to move quickly not only increases our chance of being able to get a deal done if we want to, but it makes it so we don't end up having to pay a lot more because the process drags out." He went on to say, "I think some companies might just take many weeks or months to review some stuff, and I think one of the things we've always prided ourselves on and one of the things that has always worked well for Facebook is that we've just been able to be flexible and move quickly on important things. And that's served us very well."

We don't see how any company preparing for the Fifth Era and recognizing that innovation is now a global and external phenomenon can do without a comprehensive acquisition program aligned with its innovation strategy. The most innovative companies all agree.

Risk	High to Low
Cost	Low to High
Implementability	Easy to Hard

So that ends the external innovation toolkit: 17 tools that we see the most innovative companies using to complement their own internal innovation activities.

As we began this chapter, so we will finish it.

The innovation leaders consistently demonstrate two characteristics when we examine their use of the external innovation toolkit. The first characteristic is the degree to which they use the 17 tools. We see the most innovative companies in the world using each of these tools on a scale and scope that is a magnitude greater than most large corporations that we observe at work. Secondly, it is the way in which they focus their external innovation strategy against their own innovation priorities. This alignment creates sharp focus but also requires a great deal of management and constant tuning up of the use of each tool to ensure it continues to perform in the ways required to drive the company's objectives.

Chapter 12
Happen to Things

It had long since come to my attention that people of accomplishment rarely sat back and let things happen to them. They went out and happened to things.

—Leonardo Da Vinci

In this final and short chapter we summarize the thesis and implications of this book.

Twice over.

Jack-of-All-Trades

In 1592 Robert Greene wrote in his book *Groats-worth of Wit* that actor-turned-playwright William Shakespeare was a jack-of-all-trades.

Greene meant to be rude to Shakespeare in that he viewed the latter as not very good at anything in particular, an amateur and a dilettante who could not go very deep in any genre of poetry or playwriting, in Greene's opinion.

Today we view Shakespeare as perhaps the greatest user of the English language. His breadth and ability to operate across genres is of course one of his most famous characteristics; tragedy, romance, comedy, sonnets, he did it all.

The fuller expression is "Jack of all trades, master of none" or even "Jack of all trades master of none is oftentimes better than master of one."

In the new corporate innovation approach, the most innovative companies are acting as if they fully believe that Greene's intended slight of Shakespeare is indeed the greatest of praise.

The most innovative companies are using a very different approach to corporate innovation, which requires focus on so many dimensions that it is hard to imagine that anyone can master any of them—let alone all of them.

But that seems to be alright. They work in all dimensions at once and incrementally make them all better over time. They are believers in scientific trespass on a global scale.

They do this because innovation is their core capability.

Innovation is the leitmotif of this time—the time of transition towards a new Fifth Era.

Master of None

To illustrate the thesis of our book with the help of the Bard of Avon, we offer this summary.

> *What is past is prologue.*

We have passed through four great eras, but we are in the time of transition towards a fifth.

> *There is a tide in the affairs of men,*
>
> *Which taken at the flood, leads on to fortune.*
>
> *Omitted, all the voyage of their life is bound in shallows and in miseries.*
>
> *On such a full sea are we now afloat.*
>
> *And we must take the current when it serves,*
>
> *or lose our ventures.*

The Fifth Era will be driven by the Digital Revolution, the Biotechnology, Revolution and a host of other disruptive innovations that are coming at a faster rate than the world has ever seen before. The most innovative companies know and passionately believe that the only way to win in this new era will be to meet new and changing customer needs as the underlying assumptions upon which all of our business and societal activities have been built become destabilized and replaced in the transition to the Fifth Era.

> *If to do were as easy as to know what were good to do,*
> *chapels had been churches,*
> *and poor men's cottages princes' palaces.*

They don't know exactly which human activity will be destabilized next, but they want to be there just as disruption opens up new economic value-creation opportunities. This is the greatest economic value-creation opportunity the world has ever seen, and those who embrace this have become the most valuable companies in the world.

> *The sudden hand of Death close up mine eye!*

Meanwhile, those that are lagging in innovation and are seemingly unable to adjust their strategies to compete with disruptive innovations are seeing enormous losses in economic value.

> *Uneasy lies the head that wears a crown.*

The most innovative companies have realized that they can't rely on the old approaches to corporate innovation that worked so well in the Industrial Era. Despite their great success to date, they know they need to change, and they have been paranoid in looking for a new approach.

Modest doubt is called the beacon of the wise.

Each of the leaders in these companies understands that to lead in a time of such fundamental change requires them as individuals to be knowledgeable and embracing of the disruptive innovations that will shape their company's future. But they are honest in recognizing what they don't know.

I say there is no darkness but ignorance.

Knowing their own failings, they each will own this and make seeking out knowledge about innovations their central task and daily homework.

A fool thinks himself to be wise,
but a wise man knows himself to be a fool.

They don't do this in isolation. As part of their corporate innovation approach they seek out those from whom they can learn, and once they have taken on board those others' understanding they internalize it through teaching and speaking it.

He goes through life, his mouth open, and his mind closed.

They change the mindset of their entire leadership team. Ensuring that innovation is a shared value is always on every agenda and is discussed every time the board and executive leadership team come together. In this way, they are making sure they change any mindset that is not open to innovation.

I must be cruel, only to be kind.

Difficult though it is, as leaders of their companies, they also know that they may have to change out longtime executives who are finding it difficult to adjust to these times of change and disruptive innovation, no matter how great the service and sacrifice that these people have made to the company in the past.

There are more things in heaven and earth, Horatio, than are dreamt of in your philosophy.

They then build new teams full of diverse people and voices to ensure that every aspect of innovation is considered and brought to the company and its products and services, not just those that are familiar or already understood.

*See first that the design is wise and just;
that ascertained, pursue it resolutely.*

With a diverse team, they then ensure that their company is building and aligning every strategy and plan with innovation at its core or woven into it. These innovation strategies are made to support every business and functional strategy, and every one of the same must fully embrace innovation. The resulting focus is driven resolutely in all that follows.

To business that we love we rise betimes,

and go to't with delight.

The leaders of these most innovative companies then ensure that they create a culture of innovation that supports their strategy, engages the entire organization in becoming passionate, spirited, and driven to accomplish that strategy, and they use the rallying cries of customer-focus and pride in competitive and innovative products and services to make this happen.

Things done well and with a care,

exempt themselves from fear.

The broad organization is used to make sure that innovation can't help but become the rallying cry. Their leaders task every employee with being passionate about making sure that the voice of the customer is heard and that unmet needs or competitive gaps are felt and considered so dreadful that everyone focuses on fixing them.

Ignorance is the curse of God;

knowledge is the wing wherewith we fly to heaven.

They give every employee a mandate to not rest if leaders are unaware of what is going on at the frontline. In turn, the employees make sure their leaders know the realities of the customer experience, and they don't rest until they see action to make problems go away.

Assume a virtue if you have it not.

These companies have fantastic innovators working within their four walls, and they try their best to imagine, develop, and launch their own homegrown disruptive innovations. But they also know that they can't do everything, and as a result, they are willing to let others bring their voices to the table: external innovators who can help drive the company forward.

Give every man thy ear.

As a result, every one of the most innovative companies in the world has a comprehensive external innovation strategy, which combines a breadth of tools that helps access other people's knowledge, insight, creativity, and innovativeness. They begin this by reaching out to the world's innovators and learning from them.

Virtue is bold, and goodness never fearful.

They then take risks on external innovators, entrepreneurs and the companies they are building, to ensure their own company has privileged access to the next wave of innovations and the products and services that are being created.

Nothing can come of nothing.

These companies are very active in the places where technology entrepreneurs and disruptive innovators are to be found, i.e., in centers of research and in incubators and accelerators, both as visitors, sponsors, and sometimes operators since every prospective innovation needs a place to begin.

Neither a borrower nor a lender be.

In addition to being prepared to take risks, as part of their new external innovation strategy they understand that they need to move beyond business as usual . . .

What a piece of work is a man,

how noble in reason,

how infinite in faculties,

in form and moving how express and admirable,

in action how like an angel,

in apprehension how like a god.

. . . and become an equity investor directly into entrepreneurial ventures and also indirectly by putting capital into those angel and venture funds that are finding and backing the technology entrepreneurs. They sometimes launch their own corporate venture funds too.

A peace is of the nature of a conquest;

for then both parties nobly are subdued,

and neither party loser.

Extending their external innovation programs even more broadly, corporate innovators consider tools that allow them to become partners and collaborators with other innovators, thus bringing these breakthroughs into supporting rather than disrupting the plans of the corporation as licensing partners, go-to-market partners, and sometimes in joint ventures.

Fishes live in the sea, as men do a-land;

the great ones eat up the little ones.

And without exception, the most innovative companies are aggressively using acquisition programs to buy up innovations and innovative people, from multibillion-dollar acquisitions, hosts of smaller purchases, and acquihires too.

Once more unto the breach

They are using every weapon in the external innovation armory in a battle to win the war for innovation supremacy.

To be or not to be

They have created and mastered a new approach to corporate innovation designed for the Fifth Era, for it is the only way they can find to be successful in a world of innovations.

Matthew C. Le Merle and Alison Davis

That was fun! We love you brainyquote.com.

O, had we but followed the arts!
—William Shakespeare

Final Thoughts

For 30 years, we have been in Silicon Valley and have been exposed to the world's leading innovation cluster. Over that time, almost by osmosis, we have observed and absorbed from others so much about this most dynamic of times. During the last two decades Alphabet/Google, Apple, Amazon.com, Facebook, and Microsoft have become the most valuable and innovative companies in the world. This book summarized what we have learned from them. To reiterate:

- The world is entering a new era: the Fifth Era.
- This is being driven by a host of disruptive innovations with the Digital Revolution and the Biotechnology Revolution central among them.
- Everything humans do is being transformed at the most fundamental of levels.
- The underlying assumptions that we built upon in the Industrial Era, and in the eras before it, cannot be taken for granted.
- Each time new disruptive technologies make an underlying assumption obsolete, they open the way for new business opportunities and for the entrepreneurs and businesses that exploit them.
- This represents the greatest economic value-creation opportunity the world has ever seen.
- The most valuable companies in the world are increasingly those that are exploiting this time . . .
- . . . and those that don't are seeing massive economic value destruction.

In order to prosper in this time of opportunity, the most innovative companies in the world are following a new more intense approach to corporate innovation. This is an approach with four elements:

1. **Drive Innovation Top-Down.** At the most innovative companies, innovation is a priority focus at the very top of the company – driven by the CEO and executive team with active interest and input from the board of directors. Innovation is driven top-down as leaders live it in their own actions and behaviors and by requiring others to understand the environment and think about and plan for the future.

2. **Embed Innovation into Strategies and Plans.** The second element is the extent to which the innovation strategy is developed into plans and actions across business. The most innovative companies give a great deal of thought to the creation and embedding of their innovation strategy into their corporate strategies and plans.

3. **Build an Innovation Culture.** The third element is the creation of a culture that supports innovation and in which every employee, from the top leadership to the functions and frontline staff, is passionate, spirited, and driven towards finding superior and innovative ways to serve customers better than their competitors do. This ensures that there is a high degree of alignment between the culture of the company and the innovation strategy.

4. **Exploit External Innovation.** The final element that makes up the new approach to innovation is a refocusing of innovation activities to ensure that they are driven externally versus internally. The most innovative companies are tapping into

the world's innovators and their innovations rather than re-lying on breakthroughs created within the four walls of their own corporations.

The good news is that this new approach is one that every company can apply to better exploit the disruptive innovations of the Fifth Era.

Now is the time for action. This exciting time of transition is creating huge opportunities and vast fortunes will be lost and gained over the next 5, 10, and 20 years. We hope you found this book helpful, and we wish you the best as you seek to prosper and thrive in the Fifth Era.

> *Better three hours too soon than a minute too late.*
> *—William Shakespeare*

References

Aguila-Obra, A., Padilla-Melendez, A., and Serarols-Tarres, C. (2007). Value creation and new intermediaries on Internet. An exploratory analysis of the online news industry and the web content aggregators. *International Journal of Information Management, 27*(3), 187–199.

Andrews, E. (2017). Is tech disruption good for the economy? Retrieved from https://www.gsb.stanford.edu/insights/tech-disruption-good-economy

Angel Resource Institute at Willamette University. (2015). Halo report—2015 annual report. Retrieved from https://angelresourceinstitute.org/reports/halo-report-full-version-ye-2015.pdf

A.T. Kearney Global Management Consulting Company (2015). *Connected risks: Investing in a divergent world. The 2015 A.T. Kearney Foreign Direct Investment Confidence Index.* Retrieved from https://www.atkearney.com/documents/10192/5797358/Connected+Risks%E2%80%94Investing+in+a+Divergent+World.pdf/e45b9ffa-700b-445e-bb34-e2dfff082009

Atkinson, R. D., Ezell, S. J., Andes, S. M., Castro, D. D., & Bennett, R. (2010). The Internet economy 25 years after .com: Transforming commerce and life. The Information Technology and Innovative Foundation. Retrieved from http://www.itif.org/files/2010-25-years.pdf

Barton, D., Chen, Y., & Jin, A. (2013). Mapping China's middle class. Retrieved from http://www.mckinsey.com/industries/

retail/our-insights/mapping-chinas-middle-class

Bilbao-Osorio, B., Dutta, S., & Lanvin, B. (Eds.). (2014). The global information technology report 2014: The rewards and risks of big data. (1st ed.). Geneva: World Economic Forum and INSEAD. Retrieved from http://www3.weforum.org/docs/WEF_GlobalInformationTechnology_Report_2014.pdf

Brookings (2016). *Accelerating growth: Startup accelerator programs in the United States.* Washington, DC: Hathaway, I. Retrieved from https://www.brookings.edu/research/accelerating-growth-startup-accelerator-programs-in-the-united-states/

Catalyst (2002). Making change: Creating a business case for diversity. Retrieved from http://www.catalyst.org/knowledge/making-change-creating-business-case-diversity

Central Intelligence Agency. (2016). The world factbook. Retrieved from https://www.cia.gov/library/publications/the-world-factbook/geos/xx.html

Childe, G. V. (1929). *The most ancient east: The oriental prelude to European prehistory.* New York, NY: Alfred A. Knopf.

Crowdnetic. (2015). Crowdnetic's quarterly private companies publicly raising data analysis. Title II turns two. Retrieved from http://www.crowdnetic.com/reports/sep-2015-report

Cumming, D., & John, S. (2014). The economic impact of entrepreneurship: Comparing international datasets. *Corporate Governance: An International Review, 22,* 162–178.

Dann, C., Le Merle, M., & Pencavel, C. (2012). The lesson of lost value. *strategy + business*. Retrieved from https://www.strategy-business.com/article/00146?gko=f2c51

Dean, D., Digrande, S., Field, D., Lundmark, A., O'Day, J., . . . Zwillenberg, P. (2012). Connected world series: The Internet economy in the G–20: The $4.2 trillion growth opportunity. The Boston Consulting Group. Retrieved from https://www.bcg.com/documents/file100409.pdf

DeGennaro, R., & Dwyer, G. (2010). Expected returns to stock investments by angel investors in groups. Retrieved from https://www.frbatlanta.org/research/publications/wp/2010/14.aspx

Deloitte LLP (2014). Foreign direct investment and inclusive growth: The impacts on social progress. Retrieved from https://www2.deloitte.com/content/dam/Deloitte/global/Documents/About-Deloitte/gx-dttl-FDI-and-inclusive-growth.pdf

De Treville, S., Petty, J., & Wager, S. (2014). Economies of extremes: Lessons from venture-capital decision making. *Journal of Operations Management, 32*(6). doi: 10.1016/j.jom.2014.07.002

Dezsö, C. L., & Ross, D. G. (2012). Does female representation in top management improve firm performance? A panel data investigation. *Strategic Management Journal, 33*(9), 1072–1089.

Dietz, L. D. (1997). The legal and regulatory environment of the Internet. *Information Systems Security, 6*(1), 55–63.

Dogsofthedow (2017). [table listing 50 largest companies by market capitalization available on major U.S. stock exchanges]. Largest companies by market cap today. Retrieved from http://dogsofthedow.com/largest-companies-by-market-cap.htm

Dow Jones VentureSource (2016). Venture capital report, U.S. 4Q 2015. Dow Jones. Retrieved from http://images.dowjones.com/wp-content/uploads/sites/43/2016/01/21024130/DJ-Venture-Source-US_4Q15-.pdf

Ernst & Young (2014). Adapting and evolving: Global venture capital insights and trends 2014. Retrieved from http://www.ey.com/Publication/vwLUAssets/Global_venture_capital_insights_and_trends_2014/$FILE/EY_Global_VC_insights_and_trends_report_2014.pdf

European Commission Joint Research Centre Institute for Prospective Technological Studies (2010). *The 2010 report on R&D and ICT in the European Union 2010*. Luxembourg: Turlea, G., Nepelski, D., de Prato, G., Lindmark, S., de Panizza, A., Picci, L., . . . Broster, D.

Farhadi, M., Ismail, R., & Fooladi, M. (2012). Information and communication technology use and economic growth. *PLoS ONE, 7*(11), e48903. doi:10.1371/journal.pone.0048903

Faria, A., & Barbosa, N. (2014). Does venture capital really foster innovation? *Economics Letters, 122* (2), 129–131.

Forbes (2009, February 19). Top 30 innovations of the last 30 years. Retrieved from https://www.forbes.com/2009/02/19/innovation-internet-health-entrepreneurs-technology_wharton.html

Friedrich, R., Peterson, M., Koster, A., & Blum, S. (2010). The rise of generation C—Implications for the world of 2020. Booz & Company. Retrieved from http://www.strategyand.pwc.com/media/file/Strategyand_Rise-of-Generation-C.pdf.pdf

Friedrich, R., Le Merle, M., Peterson, M., & Koster, A. (2011). The next wave of digitization—Setting your direction, building your capabilities. Booz & Company. Retrieved from http://www.strategyand.pwc.com/media/uploads/Strategyand-Next-Wave-of-Digitization.pdf

Friedrich, R., Peterson, M., Koster, A., Grone, F. & Le Merle, M. (2011). Measuring industry digitization—Leaders and laggards in the digital economy. Booz & Company. Retrieved from http://www.strategyand.pwc.com/reports/measuring-industry-digitization-leaders-laggards

George, L., & Hogendorn, C. (2012). Aggregators, search and the economics of new media institutions. *Information Economics and Policy, 24*(1): 40–51.

Georgiades, E. (2010). Copyright liability for users and distributors of content sharing and communication technologies: A crossroads between past and present. *Information & Communications Technology Law, 19*(1), 1–26. http://dx.doi.org/10.1080/13600831003593154

Gladwell, M. (2008). *Outliers: The story of success.* New York, NY: Little, Brown and Company.

Glover, T. (2012, March 3). Middle East angel investors daring to turn their sights homeward. The National. Retrieved from http://www.thenational.ae/lifestyle/personal-finance/middle-east-angel-investors-daring-to-turn-their-sights-homeward

Grilli, L., & Murtinu, S. (2014). Government, venture capital and the growth of European high-tech entrepreneurial firms. *Research Policy, 43*(9), 1523–1543.

GSMA (2014). The mobile economy 2014. London: UK. Retrieved from https://www.gsmaintelligence.com/research/?-file=bb688b369d64cfd5b4e05a1ccfcbcb48&download

Hobbes, T. (1651). *Leviathan.*

Ibrahim, D. (2010). Financing the next Silicon Valley. *Washington University Law Review, 87*(4), 717–762.

Jaruzelski, B., Le Merle, M., & Randolph, S. (2012). The culture of innovation: What makes San Francisco Bay Area companies different? San Francisco, CA: Bay Area Council Economic Institute. Retrieved from http://www.bayareaeconomy.org/files/pdf/CultureOfInnovationFullWeb.pdf

Kelly, E. (2006). *Powerful times: Rising to the challenge of our uncertain world.* Upper Saddle River, NJ: Wharton School Publishing.

Kende, M. (2014). Global Internet report 2014. Geneva: Internet Society. Retrieved from https://www.internetsociety.org/sites/default/files/Global_Internet_Report_2014.pdf

Kogan, L., Papanikolaou, D., Seru. A., & Stoffman, N. (2012). Technological innovation, resource allocation, and growth. National Bureau of Economic Research (NBER). doi: 10.3386/w17769

Kuhn, T. (1962). *The structure of scientific revolutions.* Chicago, IL: University of Chicago Press.

Kunstner, T., Le Merle, M., Gmelin, H., & Dietsche, C. (2013). The digital future of creative Europe—The economic impact of digitization and the Internet on the creative sector in Europe.

Booz & Company. Retrieved from http://cercles.diba.cat/documentsdigitals/pdf/E130122.pdf

Laudicina, P., & Ambani, M. (2012). *Beating the global odds: Successful decision-making in a confused and troubled world.* Hoboken, NJ: John Wiley & Sons, Inc.

Le Merle, M., & Campbell, J. (2009). Building an external innovation capability. Booz and Company. Retrieved from http://www.fifthera.com/perspectives-blog/2014/12/9/building-an-external-innovation-capability?rq=Building%20an%20external%20innovation%20capability

Le Merle, M., & Le Merle, L. (2015). Capturing the expected returns of angel investors in groups—Less in more, diversify. Fifth Era LLC. Retrieved from https://static1.squarespace.com/static/5481bc79e4b01c4bf3ceed80/t/56a1c90fdc5cb4477ee-852b9/1453443345617/2016+Fifth+Era+-+Less+in+more%2C+-Diversify.pdf

Le Merle, M., & Le Merle, Max. (2016). Do VCs back start-ups? Ensuring start-ups are backed in an innovation cluster. Fifth Era LLC. Retrieved from https://static1.squarespace.com/static/5481b-c79e4b01c4bf3ceed80/t/56d29bf2f699bb6f0be6689c/14566 43060069/2016+Fifth+Era+-+Do+VC%27s+back+start-up-s%3F.pdf

Le Merle, M., Davis, A., & Le Merle, F. (2016). The Impact of Internet regulation on investment. Fifth Era LLC. Retrieved from https://ennovate.withgoogle.com/uploaded-files/AMIfv 94dQN3_ypoQO23PVxaIcGtjEpAvj6PLGpSCDdGB-6V27k8lb-ubTMAHHrX_EClE3U4RRj9Zq73DkYhn-8ZIU_Iahm8IQH_aIDFHvh5mZq8KyteCBe2IyVocz1o8iCy-8FTGAKF_NCitY8dyP4JyNMnXNIU7OcU1vxtJ4pEpJZY-

WS00nvNAYEs

Le Merle, M., Le Merle, T., & Engstrom, E. (2014). The impact of Internet regulation on early stage investment. Fifth Era LLC. Retrieved from https://static1.squarespace.com/static/5481bc79e4b01c4bf3ceed80/t/5487f0d2e4b08e455df8388d/1418195154376/Fifth+Era+report+lr.pdf

Le Merle, M., & Michels, N. (2013). Taking action for tomorrow—California life sciences strategic action plan. Governor of the State of California, Bay Area Council, BayBio & Monitor Group. Retrieved from http://www.fifthera.com/perspectives-blog/2014/12/9/taking-action-for-tomorrow-bay-area-life-sciences-strategic-action-plan

Le Merle, M., Sarma, R., Ahmed, T., & Pencavel, C. (2011a). The impact of EU Internet copyright regulations on early-stage investment. Booz & Company. Retrieved from http://docs.media.bitpipe.com/io_10x/io_102267/item_485931/Booz&Co%20The%20Impact%20of%20E%20U%20%20Internet%20Copyright%20Regulations%20on%20Early-Stage%20Investment%20A4%2012-15-2011v6.pdf

Le Merle, M., Sarma, R., Ahmed, T., & Pencavel, C. (2011b). The impact of EU Internet privacy regulations on early-stage investment. Booz & Company. Retrieved from http://www.strategyand.pwc.com/media/uploads/Strategyand-Impact-EU-Internet-Privacy-Regulations-Early-Stage-Investment.pdf

Le Merle, M., Sarma, R., Ahmed, T., & Pencavel, C. (2011c). The impact of U.S.Internet copyright regulations on early-stage investment. Booz & Company. Retrieved from http://www.strategyand.pwc.com/media/uploads/Strategyand-

Impact-US-Internet-Copyright-Regulations-Early-Stage-Investment.pdf

Le Merle, M., Sarma, R., Ahmed, T., & Pencavel, C. (2011d). The impact of U.S. Internet privacy regulations on early-stage investment. Booz & Company.

Lerner, J., Schoar, A., Sokolinski, S., & Wilson, K. (2016, February 28). The globalization of angel investments: Evidence across countries. Working paper 16–072. Retrieved from http://www.hbs.edu/faculty/Publication%20Files/16-072_95a38a8a-37e5-4ee2-aa76-9eaee7e5162b.pdf

Maddison, A. (2007). *Contours of the world economy 1–2030 AD: Essays in macro-economic history.* Oxford, U.K.: Oxford University Press.

Marsden, T. C. (2012). Internet co-regulation and constitutionalism: Towards European judicial review. *International Review of Law, Computers & Technology, 26,* 2–3.

Mason, C. M., & Harrison, R. T. (2002). Is it worth it? The rates of returns from informal venture capital investments. *Journal of Business Venturing, 17*(3), 211–236.

Mason, C. M., & Harrison, R. T. (2011). Annual report on the business angel market in the United Kingdom: 2009/10. Retrieved from https://www.gov.uk/government/uploads/system/uploads/attachment_data/file/32218/11-p116-annual-report-business-angel-market-uk-2009-10.pdf

May. B., Chen, Jeng-Chung, V., & Wen, K. (2004). The differences of regulatory models and Internet regulation in the European Union and the United States. *Information & Communications*

Technology Law, 13(3), 259–272.

May, J., & Liu, M. (Eds.). (2016). *Angels without borders: Trends and policies shaping angel investment worldwide.* Singapore: World Scientific Publishing Company.

McCahery, J., & Vermeulen, E. (2014). Conservatism and innovation in venture capital contracting. *European Business Organization Law Review, 15*(2), 235–266. doi: https://doi.org/10.1017/S1566752914001116

Musyoka, C. (2015). Governments in Africa: Let's support angel investors, key drivers of entrepreneurship. Venture Capital 4 Africa. Retrieved from https://vc4a.com/blog/2015/09/07/governments-in-africa-lets-support-angel-investors-key-drivers-of-entrepreneurship/

National Center for Education Statistics (n.d.). Fast facts: Back to school statistics. Retrieved March 26, 2017, from https://nces.ed.gov/fastfacts/display.asp?id=372

National Venture Capital Association (2013). Venture capital review, Issue 29, Arlington, VA: NVCA. Retrieved from http://www.ey.com/Publication/vwLUAssets/PDF-Venture-Capital-Review-Issue-29_2013/$FILE/Venture-Capital-Review-Issue-29_2013.pdf

National Venture Capital Association (2014). NVCA 2014 yearbook. Arlington, VA: NVCA.

National Venture Capital Association (2015). NVCA 2015 yearbook. Arlington, VA: NVCA.

O'Brien, D. (2008). Copyright challenges for user generated intermediaries: Viacom v YouTube and Google. In B. Fitzgerald, F. Gao, D. O'Brien, & S. Xiaoxiang Shi (Eds.), *Copyright law, digital content and the Internet in the Asia-Pacific* (pp. 219–234). Sydney, Australia: Sydney University Press.

OECD (2011). *Financing high-growth firms: The role of angel investors*. Paris: OECD Publishing.

OECD (2012). *Internet economy outlook 2012*. Paris: OECD Publishing.

OECD (2013). *Entrepreneurship at a glance*. Paris: OECD Publishing.

Pélissié du Rausas, M., Manyika, J., Hazan, E., Bughin, J., Chui, M., & Said, R. (2011, May). Internet matters: The net's sweeping impact on growth, jobs, and prosperity. McKinsey Global Institute. Retrieved from http://www.mckinsey.com/industries/high-tech/our-insights/internet-matters

Perset, K. (2010). The economic and social role of Internet intermediaries. OECD. Retrieved from https://www.oecd.org/internet/ieconomy/44949023.pdf

Porter, M. (1990). *The competitive advantage of nations*. New York, NY: The Free Press.

Porter, M. (2000). Location, competition, and economic development: Local clusters in a global economy. *Journal of Economic Development Quarterly, 14*(1), 241–261.

PricewaterhouseCoopers & National Venture Capital Association (2014). MoneyTree™ report Q1 2014. Retrieved from https://www.pwc.com/us/en/technology/assets/pwc-moneytree-q1-2014-summary-report.pdf

PricewaterhouseCoopers & National Venture Capital Association (2015). MoneyTree™ report Q1 2015. Retrieved from http://www.pwc.com/us/en/technology/assets/pwc-money-tree-q1-2015-summary.pdf

Roach, G. (2010). Is angel investing worth the effort? A study of Keiretsu Forum. *Venture Capital, 12*(2), 153–166. doi: http://dx.doi.org/10.1080/13691061003643276

Sahlins, M. (1972). "The original affluent society." In *Stone age economics* (1–39). New York, NY: Routledge.

SBA U.S. Small Business Administration (n.d.). Small business facts and infographics. Retrieved March 26, 2017, from https://www.sba.gov/content/small-business-facts-and-infographics

Scheela, W., Isidro, E., Jittrapanun, T., & Trang, N. (2015). Formal and informal venture capital investing in emerging economies in Southeast Asia. *Asia Pacific Journal of Management, 32*(3), 597–617. doi: 10.1007/s10490-015-9420-5

Scheela, W., Isidro, E., Jittrapanun, T., Trang, N., & Gunawan, J. (2012). Business angel investing in emerging economies: Policy implications for Southeast Asia. Paper presented at Kauffman Foundation's International Research and Policy Roundtable, Liverpool, U.K., March 11–12. Retrieved from http://www.kauffman.org/~/media/kauffman_org/z_archive/resource/2012/5/irpr_2012_scheela.pdf

Schwartz, P. (1991). *The art of the long view: Planning for the future in an uncertain world.* New York, NY: Doubleday.

Schwartz, P., Leyden, P., & Hyatt, J. (2000). *The long boom: A vision for the coming age of prosperity.* New York, NY: Basic Books.

Scientific American (1913). The greatest innovations of our time. Scientific American CIX(18).

Smith, Adam. (1776). *The wealth of nations.*

Sohl, J. (2014). The angel investor market in 2014: A market correction in deal size. Center for Venture Research. Durham, NH: University of New Hampshire. Retrieved from https://paulcollege.unh.edu/sites/paulcollege.unh.edu/files/webform/2014%20Analysis%20Report.pdf

Sohl, J. (2015). The angel investor market in 2015: A market correction in deal size. Center for Venture Research. Durham, NH: University of New Hampshire. Retrieved from https://paulcollege.unh.edu/sites/paulcollege.unh.edu/files/webform/Full%20Year%202015%20Analysis%20Report.pdf

Srinivasan, S., Barchas, I., Gorenberg, M., & Simoudis, E. (2014). Venture capital: Fueling the innovation economy. *Computer, 47*(8), 40–47.

Teare, G., & Desmond, N. (2016). The first comprehensive study on women in venture capital and their impact on female founders. TechCrunch. Retrieved from https://techcrunch.com/2016/04/19/the-first-comprehensive-study-on-women-in-venture-capital/

Torchia, M., Calabrò, A., & Huse, M. (2011). Women directors on corporate boards: From tokenism to critical mass. *Journal of Business Ethics, 102*(2), 299–317.

Umeora, C. (2013). Effects of foreign direct investment (FDI) on economic growth in Nigeria. Available at http://dx.doi.org/10.2139/ssrn.2285329

United Nations (2014). World investment report 2014: Investing in the SDGs: An action plan, Geneva: United Nations, UNCTAD. Retrieved from http://unctad.org/en/PublicationsLibrary/wir2014_en.pdf

United Nations (2015a). World investment report 2015: Reforming international investment governance. Geneva: United Nations, UNCTAD. Retrieved from http://unctad.org/en/PublicationsLibrary/wir2015_overview_en.pdf

United Nations (2015b). World population prospects: The 2015 revision. Geneva: United Nations, Department of Economic and Social Affairs, Population Division. Retrieved from https://esa.un.org/unpd/wpp/publications/files/key_findings_wpp_2015.pdf

Watson, A.M. (1974). The Arab agricultural evolution and its diffusion, 700–1100. *The Journal of Economic History, 34*(1), 8–35.

Weber, R. (2009). Internet of things—Need for a new legal environment? *Computer Law & Security Review, 25*(6), 522–27.

Wiltbank, R. (2009). *Siding with the angels. Business angel investing—Promising outcomes and effective strategies.* U.K.: British Business Angels Association.

Wiltbank, R., & Boeker, W. (2007). Returns to angel investors in groups. Angel Capital Education Foundation. Retrieved from https://www.angelcapitalassociation.org/data/Documents/Resources/AngelGroupResarch/1d%20-%20Resources%20

-%20Research/ACEF%20Angel%20Performance%20Project%2004.28.09.pdf

World Economic Forum. (2013, March). The global information technology report, 2013. Geneva: World Economic Forum. Retrieved from https://www.weforum.org/reports/global-information-technology-report-2013

World Economic Forum. (2013, August). The global competitiveness report, 2013–2014. Geneva: World Economic Forum. Retrieved from https://www.weforum.org/reports/global-competitiveness-report-2013-2014

World Economic Forum (2014, April). Delivering digital infrastructure: Advancing the Internet economy. Geneva: World Economic Forum. Retrieved from http://www3.weforum.org/docs/WEF_TC_DeliveringDigitalInfrastructure_InternetEconomy_Report_2014.pdf

Zwillenberg, P., Field, D., & Dean, D. (2014). Connected world series: Greasing the wheels of the Internet economy. The Boston Consulting Group. Retrieved from https://www.icann.org/en/system/files/files/bcg-internet-economy-27jan14-en.pdf

About the Authors

Matthew C. Le Merle

 Matthew Le Merle is co-founder of Fifth Era (www.fifthera.com) and managing partner of Keiretsu Capital, the world's largest angel network and most active US venture investor. For more information go to www.matthewlemerle.com.

Matthew is a sought-after speaker and innovation consultant. He is an expert on digitizaMatthew is a sought-after speaker and innovation consultant. He is an expert on digitization and technology transformations having advised leading companies including Bank of America, eBay, EDS, Gap, Genentech, Google, HP, Microsoft, PayPal and Tata/JLR and many other companies on innovation-related issues.

Matthew has advised sovereign and regional economic entities on issues of innovation, entrepreneurialism and cluster growth. Clients have covered the globe from China, the EU, and the UK to the US including in his home state of California and the Bay Area/Silicon Valley.

Matthew's career has spanned being a global strategy advisor, professional services firm leader, corporate operating executive, private equity and venture capital investor, and board director for high growth public and private digital economy companies.

Earlier in his career, Matthew spent 21 years as a strategy consultant and advisor to Fortune 500 CEOs, boards and executive teams with McKinsey & Company, and as a practice leader with EDS/A.T. Kearney and Monitor Group where he led both firms' West Coast practices and at Booz & Company. He was also a corporate executive at Gap Inc. where he was SVP strategy and corporate development and SVP global marketing.

Matthew received a B.A. (Double First) and Master's from Christ Church, Oxford, and an MBA from the Stanford Graduate School of Business. He was born in London, UK, and is now a dual US/UK citizen and lives in the San Francisco Bay Area with his wife, Alison Davis, and their five children.

Alison Davis

Alison Davis is co-founder of Fifth Era (www.fifthera.com). She is a global strategist, finance professional, public company board director and active investor in growth companies. For more information go to www.alisondavis.com.

Alison is currently a director of Royal Bank of Scotland (RBS), Fiserv (FISV), Unisys (UIS) and Ooma (OOMA), and is chair of the advisory board for BlockChain Capital. She is a former director of City National Bank (CYC), Diamond Foods (DMND), First Data Corporation (FDC), Xoom (XOOM), and many private companies and was the Chairman of LECG (XPRT) until its sale in 2011. She has chaired audit, compensation, and governance committees and is a frequent speaker on corporate governance.

Alison was previously the managing partner of Belvedere Capital, a private equity firm focused on investing in US banks and financial services firms. Prior to this, Alison was the Chief Financial Officer of Barclays Global Investors (now BlackRock), the world's largest institutional investment firm with more than $1.5 trillion of assets under management. Earlier in her career, Alison spent 14 years as a strategy consultant and advisor to Fortune 500 CEOs, boards and executive teams with McKinsey & Company, and as a practice leader with A.T. Kearney where she built and led the global Financial Services Practice.

Alison is active in the community supporting non-profits and social enterprises as a board director, fundraiser and volunteer. She has been frequently named to the "Most Influential Women in Business" list by the *San Francisco Business Times*. She received a B.A. Honors and a Master's in Economics from Cambridge University in England, and an MBA from the Stanford Graduate

School of Business after completing the first-year at Harvard. She was born in Sheffield, UK, is now a dual US/UK citizen and lives in the San Francisco Bay Area with her husband, Matthew C. Le Merle, and their five children.

About Fifth Era

Fifth Era invests in and incubates early stage technology-enabled companies. The managing team also advises companies and conducts development initiatives to support innovation and growth strategies. For more information go to **www.fifthera.com**.

MANAGEMENT TEAM
Fifth Era is led by co-founders Matthew C. Le Merle and Alison Davis, globally recognized thought leaders in digital technologies, banking, governance and investment strategies.

INVESTMENT
Fifth Era Capital Fund 1 was formed in 2005 and has invested in 42 companies and exited 11 investments to date.

Fifth Era's managing partner is also managing partner of Keiretsu Capital, the exclusive worldwide fund partner of the world's largest angel network and the most active venture investor in the US.

ADVISORY
Fifth Era works with boards and executive teams of advisory clients to set strategies, identify, conceptualize and launch new businesses, penetrate new markets and drive the corporate growth agenda.

Expertise includes:

- Corporate strategy including facilitation of boards and executive teams
- Mergers and acquisitions, joint ventures, IPOs and fundraising
- Business unit strategy with an emphasis on growth
- Innovation strategy and cultural alignment
- External innovation, collaborative innovation and ecosystem development
- Public and private dialog and business advocacy
- Regulatory policy that stimulates innovation and business formation

PARTNERS

Fifth Era partners with incubators, accelerators and investors as well as worldwide research firms that have the capabilities to provide real-time information and perspective on the issues that concern clients, investors and portfolio companies. The firm maintains an international panel of Internet technology investors and founders.

Acknowledgments

This book draws heavily upon everything we have learned as members of the remarkable San Francisco Bay Area early-stage investment community and all of its participants. For 30 years, we have been around you and you have continuously shared with us new and interesting ideas and insights. We are always surprised by the innovation, optimism, and zeal that greet us every day as we spend our time with you. Thank you.

A special thank you goes to all the people at the most innovative companies – Alphabet/Google, Amazon, Apple, Facebook and Microsoft – that we have worked with and collaborated with over the last two decades. Most of this book is built upon your creativity and passion for innovation and for making your companies as great as possible. We have learned a great deal from you. We would also like to thank the many other innovative companies that have provided insights and learnings that are also incorporated into this book. Earlier in our careers we were able to benefit greatly at McKinsey and AT Kearney from the innovation methodologies and project experiences that we had exposure to, and Matthew's time at Monitor Group and Booz & Company allowed for further refining and sharpening these perspectives.

As angels investors at Keiretsu Forum, Band of Angels, and with the Angel Capital Association of America, we have benefited from the collaborative approach to investing in which we all come together to share our deals, conduct team-based due diligence, and then work together to help our entrepreneurs be successful. We are particularly indebted to our partners at Keiretsu Capital, Randy Williams, who founded Keiretsu Forum 17 years ago, and Nathan McDonald, who is chairman of Keiretsu Forum North-West. To these active angel investors we would add additional call-outs: Ian Sobieski and Sonja Markova at Band of Angels and to all the team and angel members of both organizations. At the ACA we would like to explicitly thank Professor Robert Wiltbank, who continues to provide insights into the angel movement through his always-informative research. Other important researchers we have relied upon are detailed in the reference section of this book: we have learned greatly and borrowed significantly from your insights.

Among venture capitalists, we have learned most by watching those general partners whom we have worked with on boards: Michael Moritz and Roelof Botha of Sequoia Capital, Dick Kramlich of NEA, Warren Weiss of Foundation Capital, Keith Rabois of Khosla Ventures, Neal Dempsey of Bay Partners, Cameron Lester of Azure stand out as having been very important in our learning journey. Among stand-alone incubators and accelerators we have found the progress and impact of Rocketspace (Duncan Logan), Runway (Max Shapiro), WeWork (Adam Neuman), and YCombinator (the team) particularly instructive, and the Google Launchpad and Accelerator teams under Roy Glasberg and the Microsoft BizSpark team under Dan'l Lewin have shown us how to positively impact the lives of hundreds of technology entrepreneurs.

Turning to the technology entrepreneurs themselves, there have been so many along the way that to choose a few might be unfair. Plus, we have learned just as much from the failures in which the aspirations and optimism of the founders turned out to be misplaced as from the successes. Disruptive innovations begin with you and your vision: you are the lead actors in this play.

As to the writing of the book, Matthew C. Le Merle and Alison Davis authored this report, and all errors and omissions are theirs alone. Mark Leonard was our publisher and gave us the confidence to complete the large undertaking of putting our thoughts and perspectives into a book. Nancy Pile was our editor, and Tom Shalvarjian of 3x3 design created the exhibits throughout the book. Sue Balcer created the book interior design, and Katherine Masters designed the covers. Jennifer Bulotti is our press agent and is doing a fantastic job—thank you.

We would like to recognize the significant assistance of our Fifth Era intern team: Miles Honens, Tallulah Le Merle, Maximillian Le Merle, Louis Le Merle, Felix Le Merle, and Leonardo Le Merle, as well as Katie Hamburg and Max Navas at Keiretsu Capital, who provided additional survey results.

Finally, but by no means last, we thank our families. This book is dedicated to our parents, Joyce and Jack, and Linda and Claud with gratitude for your gift of life during this astonishing time. The future is for our children, and this book was written for them.

It took us 30 years and a lot of blind alleys and long diversions to learn what we have tried to synthesize into this book. We offer it to you in the hopes that it will be helpful as you strive to thrive and prosper in the Fifth Era.

Matthew C. Le Merle and Alison Davis
Tiburon, California, USA
April 2017

Disclaimers

Income Disclaimer

This document contains recommendations for business strategies and other business advice that, regardless of our own results and experience, may not produce the same results (or any results) for you. We make absolutely no guarantee, expressed or implied, that by following the advice in this book you will make any money or improve current profits or returns, as there are many factors and variables that come into play regarding any given business or investment strategy.

Primarily, results will depend on the nature of your due diligence, product or business model, the conditions of the marketplace, and situations and elements that are beyond your control.

As with any business endeavor, you assume all risk related to investment and money based on your own discretion and at your own potential expense.

Liability Disclaimer

By reading this document, you assume all risks associated with using the advice given herein, with a full understanding that you, solely, are responsible for anything that may occur as a result of putting this information into action in any way, regardless of your interpretation of the advice.

You further agree that neither we nor our companies can be held responsible in any way for the success or failure of your business or investments as a result of the information presented in this book. It is your responsibility to conduct your own due diligence regarding the safe and successful operation of your business or investment portfolio if you intend to apply any of our information in any way to your business or investment operations.

Terms of Use

You are given a non-transferable "personal use" license to this product. You cannot distribute it or share it with other individuals without the express written permission of the authors.

Also, there are no resale rights or private label rights granted when purchasing this book. In other words, it's for your own personal use only.

Affiliate Relationships Disclosure

We make a number of references in this book to entrepreneurs, companies, or programs that we have invested in, worked with, or recommend. We have no paid affiliate relationship at all with any entrepreneur, company, or program we reference with respect to inclusion in this book.

Stay in Touch with the Authors

Free Updates and Bonus Content!

To receive free book updates, additional content about topics covered in this book, and find out more about the authors, go to: CorporateInnovationInTheFifthEra.com

Made in the USA
Coppell, TX
27 August 2021

61243478R00173